m

Kazuo John Fukuda

Japan and China
The Meeting of Asia's Economic Giants

Pre-publication
REVIEWS,
COMMENTARIES,
EVALUATIONS . . .

"**T**his is a book that interweaves the management philosophies of the two giants in Asia—China and Japan. Through real life cases and survey findings, Fukuda explains the difficulties faced by Japanese firms in China. He also illustrates the comparative advantages of Japanese firms over U.S. and European firms in the China market. This book is not only valuable to students and academics, but is extremely valuable to practitioners as well. Western managers will find it helpful to read about Chinese and Japanese managers. Chinese and Japanese managers will find the book helpful in understanding the subtle differences underlying the business practices that they face in their daily life.

If you want to know why Japanese firms are more successful in China than their Western counterparts, this is the book that you cannot miss."

Lau Ho-Fuk, PhD
Professor and Chairman,
Department of International Business,
The Chinese University of Hong Kong

More pre-publication
REVIEWS, COMMENTARIES, EVALUATIONS . . .

"**F**acing the worst economic crisis since the 1940s, Asians have lost not only their fortune but their confidence in 'The East Asian Miracle.' Dr. Kazuo John Fukuda's book *Japan and China: The Meeting of Asia's Economic Giants* is unquestionably timely. It can serve as a resolution to the troubled souls looking for ways to sustain their faith in the miracle. 'Change or perish' as suggested by the author is indeed the only solution for East Asia. With Japan and China joining forces, their close ties and healthy rivalry would help these two countries as well as other East Asian countries economically well into the twenty-first century."

Locky K. L. Chu
Executive Director,
APAC Ind. Co. Ltd.,
Hong Kong

"**T**his is a very compact yet comprehensive basic textbook for anyone in academia, politics, or business interested in the past, present, and future of Japan and China. The author proves that each country needs the other for their respective survival and growth, although there are many differences and difficulties between them. This book is a must for everyone who has a stake of any kind in Asia.

The book provides both an objective theoretical framework and useful practical examples. It implies that doing business internationally in Asia is indeed beyond a mere counting of dollars or yuan or yen. It is a long-awaited analysis made possible only by an experienced China-observer like Dr. Fukuda."

Hideo Inohara
Professor of Cross-Cultural Management,
Sophia University,
Tokyo, Japan

"**P**rofessor Fukuda's timely book is notably authoritative, based on his exceptionally relevant personal and professional background. The book is well organized, concise, and a nice balance of scholarship and personal touches. I have known and respected John's work for years, and this is a logical culmination of much research, travel, and personal experiences. Consequently, the book is at once credible and comprehensive, yet focused and fun to read."

Warren Briggs, PhD
Professor and Chair,
Computer Information Systems,
School of Management,
Suffolk University,
Boston, MA

Japan and China
The Meeting of Asia's Economic Giants

INTERNATIONAL BUSINESS PRESS
Erdener Kaynak, PhD
Executive Editor

New, Recent, and Forthcoming Titles:

Japan and China
The Meeting of Asia's Economic Giants

Kazuo John Fukuda

International Business Press
An Imprint of The Haworth Press, Inc.
New York • London

Published by

International Business Press, an imprint of The Haworth Press, Inc., 10 Alice Street, Binghamton, NY 13904-1580

Cover design by Jennifer M. Gaska.

Library of Congress Cataloging-in-Publication Data

Fukuda, K. John (Kazuo John)
    Japan and China : the meeting of Asia's economic giants / Kazuo John Fukuda.
       p.   cm.
    Includes bibliographical references and index.
    ISBN 0-7890-0417-8 (alk. paper).
    1. Japan—Foreign economic relations—China. 2. China—Foreign economic relations—Japan. 3. Investments, Japanese—China. 4. Management—Japan. 5. Management—China. I. Title.
HF 1602.15.C6F85 1998
337.51052—dc21

                             98-12797
                             CIP

To my wife, Minnet Hsia Fukuda, with the hope
that China and Japan can prosper together
as good partners

ABOUT THE AUTHOR

K. John Fukuda, PhD, is Professor in the Department of International Business at the Chinese University of Hong Kong. He presently teaches such courses' as International Business, Asian Business, and Japanese Management. Dr. Fukuda has worked for both Japanese and American firms and has more than twenty years' experience researching the transferability of technology across national and cultural boundaries. He is the author of two books, *Japanese-Style Management Transferred: The Experience of East Asia* (1988) and *Japanese Management in East Asia and Beyond* (1993), and his work has appeared in such journals as the *International Studies of Management and Organization, International Executive,* and the *Journal of General Management.* In addition, Dr. Fukuda is a member of the Academy of International Business and the Association of Japanese Business Studies.

CONTENTS

Preface

I was born of Japanese parents and raised as a Japanese in Japan. This should certainly make me a "real" Japanese as generally defined by the Japanese themselves. However, having spent the last thirty-six years away from the homeland, first in America and then in Hong Kong, chances are I would be considered by my fellow Japanese as a "*henna Nihonjin*" (strange Japanese), who looks Japanese but thinks and even behaves like *gaijin* (foreigners). Although I might have lost my cultural uniqueness as a Japanese, I have gained multicultural richness through years of living abroad.

For more than fifteen years, I have been investigating the transferability of Japanese-style management to East Asia. During that period, I visited mainland China frequently and built up *guanxi* (connections) with people in business and academe, who became the sources of firsthand information about China's rapid economic and social changes. By luck, I was in the right place at the right time and personally witnessed China's opening up to the world (December 1978) and then Hong Kong's return to Chinese rule (July 1997). Concurrently, I also watched and followed Japan's economic advance into China.

This is a book about Japan and China—two great Asian countries in their own rights, which are bound by a common cultural heritage, yet vastly different in many respects. At the moment, both countries are experiencing economic, social, and political reforms of an unprecedented scale. In the process of making reforms, they are casting aside their differences and working together to gain an equal footing with the industrialized West, economically and politically. To determine the global roles Japan and China could play in the coming century, we must first understand Sino-Japanese relations in the context of the Asian region as a whole.

Spanning from Japan in the north to Indonesia in the south, East Asia is populated by more than 1.7 billion people whose cultures, politics, and economies differ as widely as the topographies of their countries. East Asia contains the world's second largest economy (Japan), which is now struggling to maintain its position as the economic superpower; the world's most populous country (China), which is fighting to become the next economic superpower; a tiny oil-rich sultanate with a population of only 300,000 (Brunei); and perhaps the world's last stronghold of "pure" capitalism (Hong Kong), whose sovereignty was just returned to China after more than 150 years of British colonial rule.

Despite diversities, the region's most dynamic economies share a common aptitude for melding new Western technologies with old Oriental virtues—diligence, discipline, and patience. Following in the footsteps of Japan, which rose to the rank of a world economic superpower in the 1960s, Asia's so-called "Four Little Tigers" (South Korea, Taiwan, Hong Kong, and Singapore) announced their economic coming of age in the 1970s. Today, they are joined by a new generation of "Four Baby Tigers" (Indonesia, Thailand, Philippines, and Malaysia) and, last but not least, the "Wakening Dragon" (China).

In 1950, following decades of war and turmoil, the Asian share of the world economy was a mere 17 percent. In the last three decades, Asia's rapid economic growth propelled this share to almost 40 percent. The crises in the region's currency and equity markets during the second half of 1997 created yet another turmoil throughout Asia. Still, it is expected that East Asia will be producing more than half of the world's income some time in the early decades of the next century. If in fact that happens, the balance of world economic power would further shift from the West to the East.

In the mid-1990s, foreign direct investment (FDI) in East Asia accounted for 60 percent of the world total capital flows, with Japan the biggest supplier of investment capital. China, already the second largest recipient of FDI, is expected to overtake the United States as the world's number one recipient before the turn of this century. As foreign firms compete aggressively to capture the lion's share of potentially the world's largest consumer market, China is fast emerging as the economic power that might directly threaten Japan's once dominant position in Asia.

At the 1984 Summer Olympics in Los Angeles, Japan and China won thirty-two medals each. However, twelve years later, at the 1996 Summer Olympics in Atlanta, Japan won only fourteen medals and ranked eighteenth in final medal standings, well behind the fourth-ranked China, which won forty-nine medals. As China ascends the ranks of world sports, its fast-growing economy also continues to improve and is widely expected to become the world's largest as early as the year 2010. In the past two decades, China has introduced numerous economic and social reforms, while maintaining the political power of the Communist Party.

On February 19, 1997, Deng Xiaoping, who had presided over one of the greatest revolutions of modern times, passed away at the age of ninety-three. When his economic reforms began in 1978, about 250 million people in China—almost equivalent to the whole population of the United States—lived in what was defined by international standards as absolute poverty. Within ten years, this number had fallen by 150 million—the equivalent of the combined population of Philippines, Thailand, and Malaysia. Deng Xiaoping had succeeded in changing China on a grand scale, and his successor, President Jiang Zemin, announced that in the post-Deng era, continuity without change would be the country's priority.

By contrast, there are signs that Japan's economic dominance might have reached its peak, and its relative position could well be on a long downward slide. After more than four decades of rapid economic growth, the world's second largest economy is now in deep trouble. However, it may be premature to drop Japan from the rank of a world economic superpower. In the face of recent economic woes, Japanese firms are increasing the pace of internationalization through FDI. They have also shifted the main focus of their overseas investments from North America and Europe to East Asia, with China as the main recipient. By the early 1990s, China, when combined with Hong Kong, had become the second most popular destination of Japanese FDI as well as Japan's second largest trading partner, following the United States.

A glimpse of China's management practices today indicates that the country is in dire need of management reforms. The Chinese acknowledge backwardness in their management systems and are turning to the outside world for help. People native or foreign to Japan generally believe that the effectiveness of human resource management has been the key to Japanese firms' success in maintaining competitiveness. It was therefore quite natural that many Japanese firms attempted to employ their own way of management in China. However, the transfer of Japanese-style management, even to a culturally similar country, proved to be much more difficult than expected.

At the moment, Japan is at the crossroads—economically, socially, and politically. For a country struggling to get back on track, a call for "change or perish!" has offered a real challenge. Although most Japanese agree that changes are necessary, strong feelings of cultural uniqueness persist as enduring characteristics of Japanese society. Some are convinced that the Japanese should turn to the very roots of their culture as the source of light and strength. However, the old Japan is fast disappearing. Today, members of a new generation of Japanese, freed of traditional cultural values, are increasingly taking charge of their country's drastic transformations toward creating the new Japan.

The Chinese have a long memory of Sino-Japanese military conflicts (1894-1895; 1937-1945), and they are fearful that Japan will once again become a military superpower. On the other hand, the Japanese are fearful that China will become an economic superpower, especially now with the emergence of "Greater China." In spite of fear, distrust, and suspicion toward each other, there are expectations on both sides that close ties and a healthy rivalry would help both countries enhance their opportunities to play greater roles, economically and politically, in Asia and the world, well into the twenty-first century.

Kazuo John Fukuda

Acknowledgments

Many people have directly and indirectly contributed to this book. In particular, I must thank my two mentors for generously providing me with opportunities to experience and learn different cultures and management strategies: Nobunori Shigezaki, President of Shibaden in Tokyo, who enabled me to study firsthand the American way of management at Columbia Graduate School of Business; and S. Gordon Redding, former Dean of Hong Kong University Business School, who guided and inspired me to enter the intricate field of cross-cultural management.

I thank the colleagues whose paths I have crossed in my thirty years of career employment for sharing their knowledge and experience with me. My special thanks to Professor Kin Chok Mun, Director of the Executive MBA Program at Chinese University of Hong Kong, for his support and encouragement. I am deeply indebted to Erdener Kaynak, Executive Editor; Peg Marr, Senior Production Editor; Andrew Roy, Production Editor; and Susan T. Gibson, Administrative Editor, at The Haworth Press for undertaking and guiding this book project through to completion.

The credits for the book are shared by all; the shortcomings remain my responsibility. I thank each and every one of these people. Mostly, however, I am grateful to my wife, Minnet. She is the one who first introduced and then connected me to China and its people. I thank Minnet for her help, understanding, and patience, without which I could not have passed through the many transitions that led to the completion of this book.

Chapter 1

China and Japan

- By the middle of the 1980s, the Asian side of the Pacific came of age. As it steps out of the shadow of Western dominance, there are signs that the economic center of gravity will shift from the West to Asia.
- The economy of China, the country largely dismissed as the "sick man of Asia" until very recently, is on the rise. This country could soon rank among the economic giants of the world.
- For seven long years since the bubble of its booming economy burst, Japan has been plagued by the worst recession in the postwar period. Consequently, its once dominant position could be on the decline.

ASIA ON THE MOVE

Almost a century ago, former U.S. Secretary of State John Hay said that the Atlantic was the "ocean of the present" and the Pacific would be the "ocean of the future." That forecast appears to be coming true. This could be well signified by the Asia-Pacific Economic Cooperation (APEC) established in 1988 to boost economic growth in the Asia-Pacific region. Since the first meeting hosted by Australia in 1989, APEC's membership has expanded to eighteen countries that now include the world's two largest economies, the United States and Japan, and economies as small as Papua New Guinea and Brunei. Although twelve East Asian countries (Japan, South Korea, China, Taiwan, Hong Kong, Thailand, Malaysia, Singapore, Philippines, Brunei, Indonesia, and Papua New Guinea) constitute a two-thirds majority, six non-Asian countries (United States, Canada, Mexico, Chile, Australia, and New Zealand) are also represented.

As a whole, APEC encompasses the world's largest and fastest growing economies on both sides of the Pacific Ocean, with more than one-third of the world population and nearly three-fifths of the world economy. It proved very difficult to find a common ground among these nations of diverse economies and cultures. But, significant progresses were made in the last four years. At APEC's 1994 meeting held in Indonesia, members set a goal of free and open trade and investment in the region by 2010 for industrialized economies and 2020 for developing economies. Subsequently, the Osaka Action Agenda was formulated at their 1995 meeting in Japan. And in 1996 in the Philippines, members adopted the Manila Action Plan for Asia-Pacific Cooperation, which would set going a series of actions for free trade and investment from January 1, 1997.

The available statistics show that China has been the world's largest economy for most of recorded history. The country had the highest per capita income until around 1500, and as recently as 1830, it accounted for 30 percent of the world's manufacturing output. China was the largest economy in the world until the mid-1800s, when it was overtaken by Britain. For a period of more than 500 years following the Renaissance (fourteenth to sixteenth centuries) and especially after the Industrial Revolution (eighteenth to nineteenth centuries), the West had an overwhelming influence on the world—economically as well as politically and culturally. The fate of Asia, it is fair to say, hung on the decisions and actions of the West; Asia existed on the periphery, so much so that East Asia was, and still is, called the "Far East."

Britain dominated the world economically during the Victorian era in the nineteenth century, only to be replaced by the United States in the twentieth century. The Cold War rivalry between the United States and the Soviet Union (1945-1989) ensured American hegemony in world economy. However, even before the end of that forty-five years of hostility and military tension, American dominance began to decline. In the past decade, the world has seen: (1) the collapse of Communism as a political system, which elevated the importance of open economic competition almost irrespective of political ideology; and (2) the collapse of socialism as an economic system, which fostered the global acceptance of the capitalist, market-based economic system (Halliday, 1995).

As the Cold War was brought to an end, a primarily bipolar world was replaced by a tripolar world with three major economic regions—the United States, Europe, and Asia. Although there is a general acceptance of market-based economic systems in all regions, distinct models of capitalism exist. The U.S. model highlights the primacy of market forces and processes. This is contrasted with European capitalism that highlights the welfare role of the state. Asia shares a further variant of capitalism—one that emphasizes the role of the state in industrial policy and economic development (Fitzgerald, 1996).

It is widely suggested that in the next twenty-five years, there will occur the greatest shift in economic power of more than a century. The industrialized nations that have long dominated the world economy are likely to be dwarfed by the newly industrializing nations. If the economic growth differentials that have existed during the last two decades between the developed and the developing countries persist, the share of world economic output of rich industrialized nations is expected to fall from about 60 percent in 1990 to 40 percent in 2020. On the other hand, the share of developing countries will increase from about 40 percent to 60 percent during the same period. The radical change is being brought about, in part, by the quickening pace of economic development.

Since 1965, the developing countries of East Asia have set records for the pace of economic development. South Korea, Taiwan, Hong Kong, and Singapore raised their per capita income levels more than sixfold between 1965 and 1995. Indonesia, Malaysia, and Thailand more than tripled their income levels in the same period. Then, in the summer of 1997, the currency crisis suddenly erupted in Thailand and then spread rapidly to neighboring countries, and the turmoil in the region's currency and equity markets are casting doubt on these achievements. Is this the end of the East Asian miracle?

At the 1997 World Bank meeting held in Hong Kong amid the Asian economic crises, the Bank's regional manager for strategy and partnership named reforming the financial sector a top priority for Asia. He believes that East Asian economies are fundamentally strong and have the capacity to address the institutional problems exposed by the recent turmoil. Jeffrey Sachs of the Harvard Institute for International Development shows similar optimism (Sachs, 1997). He believes that the East Asian economies can continue to muster annual GDP growth of around 5 percent per year during the coming decade. In 1993, the total gross domestic product (GDP) of East Asia was U.S. $5.5 trillion—$6.0 trillion for the NAFTA (North American Free Trade Agreement) countries of the United States, Canada, and Mexico and $6.5 trillion for the European Community (EC). Growing at a relatively moderate but still higher rate than other regions, East Asia would be a $9.0 trillion economy by the year 2005, compared with $8.0 trillion for the EC and $7.8 trillion for the NAFTA countries (Kohut, 1994).

As we move toward the next century, there are indeed signs that the economic center of gravity is shifting from the West to Asia. As early as 1983, transpacific trade exceeded transatlantic trade; in 1991, trade within East Asia overtook transpacific trade;

in 1995, Japan exported more goods to its Asian neighbors than to the United States and Europe combined. *Time*'s 1993 special issue on the Pacific Rim reported, "With the apparent drawing of the Pacific Age years ahead of schedule, East Asia will continue to set the world pace for prosperity" (Mellor, 1993, p. 16). In his recent book, *Looking at the Sun*, American journalist James Fallows drew the prophetic portrait of Asia's economic rise and its possible political consequences (Fallows, 1995). In *Megatrends Asia*, the social forecaster John Naisbitt noted, "Asia was once the center of the world, and now the center is again returning to Asia . . . We are on the threshold of the Asian Renaissance" (Naisbitt, 1995, pp. viii, xiii).

In 1993, *The Economist* conducted a survey of twenty-two countries to determine the world's best places to live, on the basis of thirty indicators selected to measure the economic, social, cultural, and political aspects of life ("Hong Kong: Up with the Best," 1994). Switzerland won as the best place to live in the world, followed by four other European countries—Germany, Spain, Sweden, and Italy. However, in terms of economy, Japan was number one. Two other Asian countries, Hong Kong and South Korea, also ranked among the top five in this category, coming in third and fourth place, respectively. Though not included in *The Economist*'s survey, Singapore would have also ranked near the top.

The World Economic Forum, together with the Swiss-based Institute of Management Development, has been compiling the *World Competitiveness Report* since 1980. The Forum defines competitiveness as the ability of a country to create added value and to generate proportionately more wealth than its competitors in the world markets. It uses eight factors to assess a nation's overall competitiveness in business: domestic economy, government, international trade and investment, finance, infrastructure, science and technology, management, and availability/quality of human resources. In its 1994 report, which combined forty-one developed and developing economies for the first time, Singapore ranked second only to the United States in terms of domestic economic strength.

A country's competitiveness is affected by its government's economic policies. In this category, Singapore received top ranking among all countries surveyed. A recent study done by the Washington-based Heritage Foundation showed that economies with the least regulation grew the fastest. According to its 1996 "Index of Economic Freedom," Singapore was the second most economically free country in the world, just behind Hong Kong (Yuen, 1996). The rating was based on ten factors: trade policy, monetary policy, taxation, government consumption of economic output, capital flows and foreign investment, banking, wage and price controls, property rights, regulation, and black market. The Forum also gave Singapore the top mark in the category of human resources, while Japan ranked first in science and technology. To a certain degree, this could be explained by the high academic standards of the countries' people.

Singapore and Japan represent neo-Confucian societies in East Asia, where academic achievement is much prized. In 1996, half a million eighth-graders from forty-one countries took examinations sponsored by an independent cooperative of research centers. In this Third International Mathematics and Science Study, Asian students dominated the top rankings in both subjects. Leading the way in average math scores were Singapore, South Korea, Japan, and Hong Kong. Although Hong Kong students only scored just above the world average, the remaining three countries led the pack in science scores as well. In fact, these East Asian countries as a group scored high in most of the eight categories examined by the World Economic Forum.

With the presence of factors favorable to competitiveness in business, East Asia became the place where foreign investors put their money and other resources. In 1995, with a $54 billion intake, accounting for 60 percent of the world total, East Asia outstripped the rest of the world in foreign direct investment (FDI) capital flows. China received U.S. $38 billion, with Malaysia a distant second at nearly $6 billion and Indonesia attracting just under $5 billion. The only non-Asian country coming close to the levels of FDI seen in the East Asian region was Mexico, which received some $4 billion.

As the region's economies and businesses race along, East Asians are climbing the ranks of the world's richest people. The roster of the world's richest people, prepared annually by *Forbes* magazine, showed that in 1996 almost 30 percent of about 450 billionaires in the world were from Asian countries. On a country-by-country breakdown, a tiny Hong Kong with twenty billionaires ranked fourth in the world behind the United States (149), Germany (52), and Japan (41). *Forbes'* latest report (Dolan, 1997) showed that Hong Kong had Asia's richest and the world's fourth richest man, as well as Asia's richest and the world's second richest woman. The combined personal fortune of Hong Kong's three richest men alone amounted to a staggering U.S. $38 billion, almost comparable to the estimated $36 billion held by Microsoft CEO Bill Gates, who was number one on the list for three consecutive years.

Reflecting on the region's resolute economic advance of the past several decades, Malaysia's Prime Minister Mahathir Mohamad regards the emergence of Asia as historically inevitable. The wheels of economic development are turning smoothly for Asia as a whole, but the rapid growth must be kept in a realistic perspective. He cautions that the economic formula that worked well in the past may not ensure Asia's place in the future. Still, he expresses optimism about the future development of Asia when he says, "We may not become the center of the world, but we should at least be the center of our part of it. We must commit ourselves to ensuring the history of East Asia will be made *in* East Asia, *for* East Asia, and *by* East Asians" (Mahathir and Ishihara, 1995, p. 16).

SUPERPOWER IN THE MAKING

China is a big country. At 3.7 million square miles, or nearly 7 percent of the world's total land area, it is slightly larger than the United States and twenty-five times larger than Japan. Its population of more than 1.2 billion, or one-fifth of the world's total, makes it the most populous country in the world. With a recorded history of more than 4,000 years that goes back to the Xia Dynasty (1994 B.C. to 1523 B.C.), the Chinese civilization is one of the oldest in the world. A succession of dynasties and warring kingdoms developed a technologically and culturally advanced society and expanded Chinese political and cultural domination throughout the Asian continent. Chinese pictographic writing, similar to that in use today, was already developed as early as 1500 B.C. during the Shang Dynasty. Ancient China also introduced paper, printing blocks, gunpowder, the magnetic compass, and countless other innovations to the world.

For centuries, the development of Chinese civilization remained largely indigenous, partly because of the independent spirit of the Chinese people and partly because of China's isolation from other civilizations. With the advent of the Age of Discovery, Portuguese and Spanish explorers and envoys began to arrive in South China in the sixteenth century, and in their wake came the traders. They wanted to trade with China, but China sought to minimize its contact with foreigners by restricting foreign trade to the port at Macao. In 1793, Lord Macartney arrived in the port city of Tianjin on a British warship to access the riches of China for trade. He was politely but firmly turned away with the Emperor's message, "We have never valued ingenious articles, nor do we have the slightest need of your country's manufactures."

The ensuing Western efforts to pry open China led to the Opium War (1840-1842), which ended with the signing of the Treaty of Nanjing and the opening of five Chinese ports. For more than 130 years from the mid-1800s to the late 1970s, Chinese history was one continuous record of humiliations and tumults—the decline and fall of a 268-year rule by the Qing Dynasty (1912), the Sino-Japanese War (1937-1945), the Civil War (1945-1949), and the Cultural Revolution (1966-1976). Until very recently, China was a weak and closed nation, largely dismissed as "the sick man of Asia." But after the death of Mao Zedong in 1976, China's door was gradually opened to the world, and new economic policies were introduced to modernize the nation's industry, agriculture, defense, and science and technology—the so-called "four modernizations."

The year 1978 became a turning point for China's economic reforms. In December of that year, Beijing officially announced "the open door policy" and began to implement its bold economic reforms in order to move China toward a market economy. Steps were taken to revitalize the nation's flagging enterprises by giving them four main rights: (1) the right to market freely part of the products, (2) the right to reserve part of the profits, (3) the right to export independently part of the products and to reserve part of the foreign exchange earnings, and (4) the right to issue bonuses at the enterprise's own discretion and to hire and dismiss employees more independently.

Many asked how such economic reforms could mesh with China's political system, which was still maintained with an iron hand by the Communist Party. "It does not matter whether the cat is black or white, as long as it catches mice." Pragmatic thinking, as expressed in this famous statement by Deng Xiaoping, the architect of China's economic reforms, presented the answer. Deng's other famous remark, "China has already gone so far in its reforms that there is no turning back," represented another aspect of his strategy for reforms. Between 1980 and the mid-1990s, China's economy grew at the annual rate of almost 10 percent, with the gross domestic product (GDP) reaching nearly U.S. $700 billion in 1995. It was the longest period of economic expansion since the establishment of the People's Republic of China in 1949.

Deng Xiaoping hoped to quadruple the nation's economy from its 1978 level to $1 trillion by the year 2000. That goal now seems highly attainable. In fact, as early as 1991, using a new method of incorporating the purchasing power of countries' currencies in calculating GDP, the International Monetary Fund (IMF) put China's economy as the third largest in the world—$1.66 trillion in GDP—after the United States and Japan. Deng's economic reforms liberalized the prices of most commodities, dramatically increased agricultural output, created booming collective and private sectors, and attracted billions of dollars in foreign investment. China's grain output soared by 60 percent from 300 million tons in 1978 to 480 million tons in 1996, making the country the world's largest agricultural producer. In the early 1990s, approximately 60 percent of the labor force was engaged in agricultural and related work, but they contributed less than 30 percent of the national income. Though less than 20 percent of the total was engaged in the industrial sector, that activity contributed more than half of the national income.

The ownership of enterprises in China has become more diverse over the last twenty years. In terms of output, the pre-1978 economy was dominated by state-owned enterprises (SOEs). Since then, the collective sector, comprising enterprises owned by communities or their own employees, has grown dramatically, and a new dynamic sector of private enterprises has also emerged. Between 1978 and 1992, the proportion of industrial output contributed by SOEs dropped from 80 percent to just under 50 percent. During the same period, the collective sector grew from 20 percent to almost 40 percent, and the private sector from 0.2 percent to nearly 7 percent (Qian and Xu, 1993).

In 1995, China's total production of goods and services (GDP) reached almost U.S. $700 billion, representing just over 15 percent of Japan's and 10 percent of the United States' GDP. Today, China ranks among the world's eight largest industrial producers—third in shipbuilding and beer production and fourth in steelmaking. The development of foreign trade has been another marked feature of the recent period. As a share of the national income, foreign trade rose from a mere 10 percent in 1978 to over 30 percent by the beginning of the 1990s. In just four years between 1993 and 1996, China's merchandise trade with the world changed from a deficit of $12 billion to a surplus of $12 billion. China now ranks among the world's eleven top traders.

In 1993, China became the second largest recipient of FDI, with investment inflow amounting to U.S. $26 billion, with the United States attracting $32 billion. In 1995, China had received more than $37 billion in FDI—more than a third of the world total; it was again second only to the United States with $60 billion. In fact, much of China's economic growth in recent years was owing to FDI, which had spurred growth in the country's productivity. During a fifteen-year period from 1979 to 1994, productivity gain accounted for more than 40 percent of China's overall economic growth; by the early 1990s, it overtook capital as the most significant source of economic growth. In fact, China's rapid economic growth is underpinned by the explosion in productivity since 1978. Research by the International Monetary Fund (IMF) showed that the country's productivity increased at nearly 4 percent a year between 1979 and 1994, compared with about 1 percent between 1953 and 1978.

Although foreign direct investment was crucial to China's productivity growth, it became even more potent when accompanied by the introduction of economic reforms in 1978 that gave profit incentives to enterprises and individuals. Liberalization in rural economy freed property rights and allowed higher prices for agricultural products, resulting in more efficient use of land and labor; greater autonomy given to enterprise managers played a key role in raising productivity. The signs of China's economic prosperity are becoming increasingly visible. Over the last seventeen years since my first visit to China, I have personally witnessed many changes that touch the daily lives of average Chinese citizens.

Thousands of acres of farmland were reclaimed to build new residential blocks, office buildings, factories, airports, highways, theme parks, golf courses, and so on. In cities and towns, *Rikishas* (rickshaws) all but disappeared, and taxis took their place as a popular means of transportation. The baggy, navy blue jackets and trousers of yesteryear largely vanished and were replaced with fashionable clothes. Posh restaurants and cafés were built in and around large cities, along with McDonald's, Kentucky Fried Chicken, and similar establishments. International-class hotels, previously off limits to locals, were built all over the country to cater not only to foreign tourists but also to Chinese guests. Private telephones, rarely seen before the mid-1980s, were installed at many households to help people get better connected with each other. And newspapers, which used to carry only limited local and national news, were now filled with international news from all over the world.

These changes have no doubt contributed to the rapid improvement of people's standard of living. However, China has been rather slow in tackling serious social problems, which have, in effect, been created by the very success of its economic reforms. The country's economic prosperity is generating a huge amount of waste; previously clean streets are now more often than not littered with trash and garbage. Once tranquil residential areas are turning into bustling commercial districts, creating noise pollution well into the night. Unchecked growth in the number of cars running on highly leaded gasoline and traffic jams caused by them are aggravating the air pollution problem. Chinese government officials are also worried about spiritual pollution, which they believe has resulted from Western cultural influence. In spite of these and other problems that they must face, top Chinese leaders realize that there is no turning back the clock; China continues to forge ahead.

Although China's economy still lags far behind the United States, Japan, and other industrialized countries in the West, there are expectations that the country will soon become an economic superpower. Lawrence H. Summers, formerly senior economist at the World Bank, noted that for more than a century, the United States has been the world's largest economy; the only nation with a chance of surpassing it in the next generation in absolute scale is China (Kristof, 1993). In its long-awaited report, *China 2020,* released in September 1997, the World Bank forecast that the Chinese economy would slow down in the years leading to 2020 with an annual growth averaging around 6.5 percent (Orr, 1997). However, at the World Economic Forum in January 1998, China's Vice-Premier Li Lanqing announced that Beijing would launch an infrastructure program to achieve 8 percent growth in the coming years. If China can indeed sustain such a high growth rate, the chances are that its economy will be the largest in the world by the year 2020.

SUPERPOWER IN TROUBLE

When Britain opened China to trade by force in 1842, it was almost a dress rehearsal for America's opening of Japan eleven years later. In the summer of 1853, six warships of the U.S. East India Fleet under the command of Commodore Matthew Perry forced their way into a small seaport near Tokyo to demand that Japan open its door to trade. It was a demand that could not be refused. Fifteen years later, Japan's modern ascent began with the sweeping reforms of the Meiji Restoration. Military defeat in 1945 brought a hard setback, but Japan bounced back to achieve one of the most dramatic half-centuries of progress that the world had ever seen.

In 1960, Prime Minister Hayato Ikeda issued a rallying cry: Japan should double its national income in ten years! Thus began the longest period of rapid economic growth in Japanese history. Throughout the 1960s, economy grew at the average of 10 percent per year, and by 1967, the national income actually doubled. Japan came of age as a modern nation in October 1964 at the opening of the eighteenth Olympic Games in Tokyo. After nearly two decades of national self-denial and hard work to climb out of the rubble of war, the country could at long last afford a $2 billion celebration. It also signaled the arrival of an economic miracle in Japan. The miracle was achieved by an ultrahigh growth driven by an explosive surge of domestic demand. This set the stage for Japan's blitz of international markets.

By the end of the 1960s, rapid industrialization had carried Japan to the rank of a world economic superpower. Futurologist Herman Kahn then proclaimed that the twenty-first century would be the "Japanese Century." However, in 1974, after hundreds of corporate bankruptcies, the country fell into a severe economic recession. This was caused by two back-to-back shocks: the "Nixon Shock" that sent the value of the yen upward by nearly 20 percent overnight, and the "Oil Shock" that pushed the price of crude oil sky high. Japanese firms quickly responded to the sudden and unexpected changes by streamlining their entire production systems. Their efforts resulted in massive export of higher value-added products, setting the stage for surges in overseas investment. As the 1970s came to an end, Harvard professor Ezra Vogel contended in his best-selling book, *Japan as Number One* (Vogel, 1979), that Japan was the world's most effective industrial power and could serve as a model for other developed countries in the West.

At the dawn of the 1980s, a yawning trade surplus began to spark resentments, fears, and charges that Japan was attempting to dominate the world economically. Fueling the "Japan bashing" was an international buying spree by Japanese firms. The end of the 1980s saw a big jump in high-stake acquisitions of some of the best-known American companies such as CBS Records, Firestone Tire and Rubber, Inter-Continental Hotels, Columbia Pictures, and Rockefeller Group. Throughout the latter half of the 1980s, Japanese economy continued to boom and expand, and as the proceeds from exports surged in, everyone went shopping. At the height of this booming economy, the value of all real estate in Japan was worth five times that of the United States!

However, the bubble finally burst in 1991; by the spring of 1992, the Japanese government all but conceded the fact of recession. For six years since, the world's second largest economy has been plagued by the worst economic recession in their postwar period. Even though Japan boasted a GDP of U.S. $4.5 trillion in 1995, as compared with $6.7 trillion for the United States, the official unemployment rate rose from 2 percent in 1990 to 3.4 percent in January 1996—the highest level in four decades. At a time when the number of management-track jobs for university graduates was declining, Japan was also suffering under a shortage of labor at the lower end of the job market. In 1950, half the population in Japan was under twenty years of age, but the number of this age group dropped to 30 percent in 1990—the result of low birth rates coupled with lowering death rates.

With more education and career opportunities available, young, independent-minded Japanese women are becoming reluctant to wed and have children. As the country celebrated Children's Day in May 1997, the government announced that Japan, with fewer children under fifteen than at any other time since the first national census in 1920, had the fastest-aging population in the world. The number of people between the ages of fifteen and sixty-four, those considered employable, is steadily shrinking (Bartholet, 1997). In 1995, 70 percent of the Japanese were in that age group; however, it is estimated that this will fall to about

60 percent in the next twenty-five years, and by then one out of every four Japanese will be sixty-five or older. This means far fewer taxpayers are supporting more and more elderly.

The Japanese government recently announced that the tax burden on individuals could become unsustainable unless the economy becomes more productive. Economists are also pointing out that if current population and productivity trends continue, there will be no improvements in the standard of living for the next twenty-five years. Japan's demographic woes will no doubt be a great burden on its economy in the coming decades. To make the problem even worse, the Japanese yen rose to historic highs against the U.S. dollar in the spring of 1995, trading at below eighty yen to one U.S. dollar—the highest level since 1971, when the fixed exchange rate of one U.S. dollar to 360 yen was abandoned. A study conducted by the Bank of Japan estimated that only a third of all Japanese firms could turn in profits at the yen-to-dollar exchange rate of between 105 and 110, and many firms reported sharp drops in profits (Richman, 1994).

The year 1995 was marked by shocking retreats by some of Japan's biggest and best-known firms, including those that had acquired large U.S. firms during the heyday of their overseas investment from the late 1980s to the early 1990s. Sony, which paid U.S. $3.4 billion in 1989 to purchase Columbia Pictures, wrote off more than $3 billion for the movie-making operations. Likewise, Matsushita sold MCA, the owner of Universal Studios, to Canada's Seagram's at $5.7 billion—nearly $400 million less than the price Matsushita paid in 1990. And, Mitsubishi Estate, which paid $846 million in 1990 to buy an 80 percent stake in New York's Rockefeller Center, was forced to give up the property when the twelve-building complex filed for bankruptcy.

The appreciation of the yen pushed the price of Japan-made products higher, resulting in steady declines in Japan's business competitiveness around the globe. In the mid-1980s, Japan replaced the longtime title holder, the United States, as the world's most competitive nation. However, it gave back the top position to the United States in 1993. And in 1996, the World Economic Forum ranked Japan in the fourth place position over-all, following the United States, Singapore, and Hong Kong. Still, in spite of general declines in competitiveness, Japan, as recently as 1994, still topped the Forum's list in terms of management. However, as Japanese firms continue to expand their overseas operations, the weaknesses of their management systems are increasingly exposed.

In September 1995, Toshihide Iguchi, a bond trader holding the third-ranking job at Daiwa Bank's New York office, was arrested by U.S. federal authorities on charges of falsifying records and concealing huge bond trading losses of more than U.S. $1 billion. Analysts were shocked by Daiwa management's cover-up of the single biggest loss in banking history and, more-over, by the fact that Japan's Finance Ministry knew about the bank's problem but did not inform U.S. banking regulators until just before Iguchi's arrest in the United States. Another aspect of the Daiwa affair that impressed the analysts was the company's apparent lack of a system for monitoring the activities of its own employees working abroad. Iguchi, who had carried out more than 30,000 unauthorized bond trades, claimed that senior Daiwa executives actually encouraged him to maintain the deception for twelve years. The scandal led to Daiwa's expulsion from U.S. financial markets, and Iguchi is now serving a four-year sentence in a U.S. jail.

Then, the news of an even bigger financial scandal broke out in the following year at Sumitomo Corporation—the world's fifth largest firm, with more than U.S. $167 billion revenues in 1995. In October 1996, the company's copper trader in London, Yasuo Hamanaka, was arrested by Japanese prosecutors after Sumitomo filed a complaint accusing him of forging documents for trading. Sumitomo put the blame for racking up losses of

$2.6 billion through unauthorized trades solely on its employee of twenty-six years. As with the Daiwa scandal, the case raised questions about Japanese authorities' ability to police the financial sector. Japanese financial regulators, however, maintained that since the trades took place overseas, it had nothing to do with the case. Hamanaka was charged with forgery and fraud—criminal offenses that could net him up to fifteen years in prison.

In March 1997, Nomura Securities, Japan's largest brokerage, disclosed yet another scandal arising from its alleged payment to *sokaiya* as compensation for trading losses. *Sokaiya* are racketeers who extort money from companies by threatening to disrupt their shareholders' meetings or by offering to prevent other *sokaiya* from interfering. Paying off *sokaiya* is a violation of Japan's commercial code. Soon after this scandal was exposed, the company's president and fifteen board members resigned. It was the second time during this decade that Nomura's top executives were forced out in the wake of scandals. In 1991, in the aftermath of the Tokyo stock market crash, Nomura Securities, along with three other "big four" brokerage firms in Japan, was alleged to have compensated its favored corporate clients for losses at the expense of smaller clients.

In fact, it has long been a common practice for Japanese brokerage firms to indemnify their important customers against losses by occasionally paying the money out of their own pockets. The Nomura affair was just one of many similar scandals to hit corporate Japan, where ties between companies and *sokaiya* racketeers and other underworld groups—*yakuza* (Japan's organized crime syndicates)—have long been a problem. In May 1997, the Nomura scandal was replayed by Dai-Ichi Kangyo Bank (DKB), Japan's third largest bank in terms of assets. DKB revealed that it had loaned a *sokaiya* U.S. $240 million without sufficient collateral, including $27 million to buy shares in Nomura and other securities firms. As soon as authorities began to search DKB offices, the bank's top managers quit, displaying the run-for-cover instinct that actually makes companies vulnerable to extortionists.

The Nomura/DKB affair is the latest stain on a Japanese financial system that has had its dirty laundry hung out in public for several years (Moffett, 1997). Back in the booming 1980s, when the stock market was strong and government regulators were pliable, the clublike securities and banking industries managed to win respect merely by keeping up a decent outward appearance. But underneath the surface, payoffs, secret deals, and insider trading were all everyday business practices. As recently as 1991, the government's survey indicated that more than 40 percent of publicly listed companies in Japan paid blackmail money to *yakuza* ("Tokyo Market Faces Cleanup," 1991). When the Japanese stock and property markets collapsed early in the 1990s, the resulting pressure on financial firms began to expose their seamier side.

Since accepting the nation's top political post in January 1996, Prime Minister Ryutaro Hashimoto has been pushing to implement much-needed financial reforms. He is determined to investigate the underlying problems and is reportedly incensed at what he called the "sneaky" resignations of Japanese executives involved in scandals before an investigation was complete. Hashimoto demanded that executives should face the truth and find out what happened. His government is hoping that through financial reforms, Tokyo can become as competitive as New York and London. Unfortunately, a series of these scandals cast a long shadow over the promotion of Tokyo as a global financial center. Although the inherent weaknesses of Japanese management are coming to light, the government is still drawing fire for failing to police financial institutions as well as itself.

The Ministry of Finance's authority, covering everything from drawing up the national budget to inspecting and supervising banks and brokerages, is the most powerful arm of the government. Unfortunately, such authority has also made the Ministry a hotbed for scandals. For example, the government-backed housing loan companies, instituted during the go-go era of "bubble economy," were alleged to have been created as landing spots for the Ministry's top officials upon their retirement. The well-connected officials, mostly with little business experience or managerial ability, did not adequately check to whom they were lending money. As a result, the housing loan companies ran up trillions of yen in bad loans through speculative property lending, some of which allegedly involving *yakuza.*

While critics were charging that loan officers were simply too afraid to collect debt from the members of *yakuza,* the Ministry went ahead and negotiated a plan to use more than 685 billion yen, or about U.S. $5.7 billion, in taxpayers' money to help liquidate housing loan companies that they themselves had created in the first place. The government of Prime Minister Hashimoto has been championing the drastic economic, financial, and social reforms to create a stronger and better Japan, but in reality, it is blamed for prolonging Japan's recession, as well as for its lack of political will to reform itself.

Chapter 2

Japan's Move into China

- To regain competitiveness in world markets, Japanese firms continue to expand their overseas production. But, the main focus has shifted from North America and Europe to Asia, with China as the priority location.
- In the past two decades, China has achieved impressive success in attracting foreign direct investment, but its continuing success calls for scores of improvements.
- Despite their cautious approach to China business, Japanese firms are now moving ahead at full steam to capitalize on China's fast-growing market and more investor-friendly environment.

FOCUS ON ASIA

After a steady economic expansion worldwide throughout the 1980s, the end of the decade saw the United States and other industrialized nations in the West slipping into a period of negative growth. While they struggled to find ways out of recession, Japan appeared insulated from the rest of the world, managing to show a slower but still positive economic growth. However, much of its economic expansion in the booming 1980s was financed by the vastly inflated value of equities and real estates. The bubble finally burst in 1991; in the following year, Tokyo's Nikkei stock index tumbled to just under 16,000—a drop of nearly 60 percent from the peak reached in December 1989. Likewise, in a five-year period from 1992 to 1997, Tokyo's real estate price fell by as much as 40 percent.

Since Japanese banks held substantial equity and real estate investments as assets, such a drastic drop in the value of stocks and properties started squeezing their lending ability. As a result, they became increasingly reluctant to extend loans to businesses. Moreover, the increasing cost of labor at home and the rising value of the yen began to hurt Japan's business competitiveness in world markets. With five decades of steady growth stifled, Japanese firms introduced a series of new strategies to cope with the mounting problems at home and abroad. By far the most important strategy was to step up the expansion of overseas production through foreign direct investment (FDI).

As recently as 1986, only about 3 percent of Japanese manufacturing was done abroad. That rose to 5 percent in 1988, compared with 21 percent for the United States and 17 percent for West Germany. It rose another point to 6 percent in the following year, according to Japan's Ministry of International Trade and Industry (MITI). A 1991 survey of some of the largest Japanese industrial firms revealed that their overseas production volume accounted for an average of 20 percent of the total manufacturing (Ishida, 1992). For example, Matsushita, the world's largest manufacturer of consumer electronics, now operates more than 150 plants in nearly forty foreign countries. And, almost half of its total sales today comes from overseas, with foreign factories supplying two-thirds of goods sold outside Japan.

Toyota, Japan's largest industrial firm and number one carmaker, operates thirty-four plants in twenty-six countries. In 1995, the company's foreign-produced vehicles accounted for about half of all its overseas sales, and Toyota is aiming to raise that to 65 percent by the end of 1998. In the fiscal year 1993, which ended in March 1994, more Japanese cars were made in the United States (1.8 million) than were imported from Japan (1.5 million) for the first time since Japan's entry into the carmaking business in the United States in the early 1980s. In 1996, Honda, the first Japanese carmaker to set up a factory in the

United States, built more cars overseas than in Japan, including some 700,000 cars in the United States alone. In 1995, for the first time ever, these and other Japanese firms together manufactured more overseas than they exported from Japan (Bartholet, 1996).

Despite such achievements, there has long been an imbalance in geographical areas where Japanese firms actually made FDI. To redress the balance, they are shifting the main focus of FDI from North America and Europe to Asia. In 1990, the Asian share of Japan's cumulative FDI worldwide was only 12 percent. It rose to 16 percent in 1992, as compared with 44 percent for North America and 20 percent for Europe. By then, well over half of new FDI by Japanese firms was in Asia—more than twice that in European Community and nearly four times more than in North America (Perry, 1992). A survey by Japan External Trade Organization (JETRO) pointed out that Asia had already replaced the United States as the focus of Japan's new FDI.

In 1993, for the first time since JETRO had started the survey of Japanese-affiliated manufacturing plants in the United States thirteen years earlier, the number of Japanese plants in the United States dropped by almost thirty to just under 1,700. Consequently, the estimated number of employees at the U.S. plants also dropped 8 percent to about 270,000 ("Number of Japanese Factories in U.S. Declines," 1994). As of March 1994, the United States still accounted for more than 42 percent of Japan's cumulative FDI of more than U.S. $420 billion worldwide, followed by Britain with 7.5 percent. China, when combined with Hong Kong, ranked fifth with 4.5 percent. However, in 1993 as a whole, China and Hong Kong together received nearly 8 percent of the total Japanese FDI, surpassing Britain's share of 7 percent. Thus, China and Hong Kong combined had pushed Britain aside to emerge as the second most popular destination for Japanese FDI.

Exported products from Japan began the foray to Asia in the 1960s; they were followed in the 1980s by Japanese investments that built factories throughout Asia—a trend that is continuing today. Japanese firms' move to Asia is supported by the government, which provides special funds to help them put together joint ventures with local businesses, insures them against commercial risks, manages a huge foreign aid program usually tied to the purchases of Japanese equipment, and so on. For example, after committing some $37 billion in Indonesia over the past three decades, Japan dominates virtually every sector of that country's industry except mining and oil extraction, which are the Americans' domain. But now, Japan is becoming more of an economic partner than a dominator in Asia.

Increasingly, Indonesia and other developing countries in Southeast Asia are becoming parts of an integrated manufacturing zone for many Japanese firms. They include: Mitsubishi Electric in Thailand (household appliances), Matsushita Electric Industrial in Malaysia (room air conditioners), Sony in Malaysia and Thailand (color televisions and compact disc players), Sumitomo Electric in Indonesia (auto wiring systems), and Iniden in Philippines (communications equipment). By the end of 1994, Japan had pumped in nearly U.S. $75 billion to the region, and it is now the single largest investor in Asia. The United States, which was neck and neck with Japan two decades ago, trailed with about $46 billion.

The reason for this eastward shift of Japanese direct investment is largely economic. Japanese firms consider that the newly industrialized economies of Hong Kong, Singapore, South Korea, and Taiwan are the most profitable places to invest, followed closely by the Association of Southeast Asian Nations (ASEAN). Some distance behind them, but ahead of Latin America, North America, and the European Community, comes China. Today, many Japanese firms have their sights set firmly on China as their priority location for FDI. They hold little concern about the transfer of the sovereignty of Hong Kong from Britain to China, which took place on July 1, 1997. Also they continue to come to Hong Kong because it is an important regional business center and the gateway to China. As recently as 1993, Japanese investment in Hong Kong increased by almost 70 percent over the previous year to U.S. $1.2 billion; another 135 Japanese companies moved into Hong Kong, taking the total to nearly 1,800, as compared with about 1,100 American firms.

INVESTING IN CHINA

FDI involves the control of a company in one country by a company from another country. Control normally means the ownership of 10 to 25 percent of the voting stocks as minimum, but even a 51 percent ownership does not always guarantee control. Besides capital, it involves a high degree of commitment of technology, personnel, and other corporate resources. To compensate for risks thus incurred, FDI should offer investors certain advantages that arise from favorable location- and firm-specific factors (Dunning, 1993). Location-specific factors include the political, cultural, and economic conditions of a foreign (host) country, while firm-specific factors include the size, organizational and management strategies, and innovatory capability of a host-country firm.

Favorable location-specific factors or location advantages imply that an investing firm finds it advantageous to locate some parts of its operations outside its home country because of the host country's government policies, resource costs, market size and growth, and so on. Favorable firm-specific factors or ownership advantages imply that a host-country firm possesses or can gain access to technology, know-how, resources, and other forms of income-generating assets that its competitors either do not possess or do not have access to. As these host-country factors evolve over time, FDI inflows to a country normally go through three distinct development stages (Dunning and Narula, 1994):

- *Beginning:* Due to inadequate domestic market, economic system, government policy, infrastructure, supply of skilled labor, and so on, the location advantages of a host country are too few to attract foreign investors. Likewise, the ownership advantages are few, as there is little or no indigenous technology of real value held by the host-country firms.
- *Growth:* FDI starts to rise as the location advantages, especially the growth of domestic market, begin to be materialized, thus making local production by foreign firms a viable proposition. The ownership advantages also increase through technology accumulation among local firms.
- *Maturity:* The growing location advantages such as a much-enlarged market and better infrastructure encourage more technology-intensive manufacturing. On the other hand, the original ownership advantages begin to erode, as local firms quickly acquire their own competitive advantages and start competing directly with foreign firms.

Only one year prior to the announcement of the Open Door Policy in December 1978, the Community Party of China proclaimed that it had never allowed, nor would it ever allow, foreign capitalists to invest in the People's Republic of China (PRC). However, the country's new constitution, drafted soon after that announcement, included an article stating that the PRC would permit foreign enterprises to invest in China and to enter into various forms of economic cooperation. This signaled a clear turnaround from the Communist Party of China's long-held policy that had shunned direct contacts with foreign capitalists.

To catch up with capitalist countries, China had turned to foreign enterprises for help. FDI began to flow into China, cautiously at first from overseas Chinese, who live outside the mainland of China, mainly in Hong Kong, Taiwan, and other Southeast Asian countries. Since 1979, it has gone through three periods of development:

1979 to 1984: The Open Door Policy was implemented, in a limited way, to do business with the outside world. In 1980, an important step was taken to establish the Special Economic Zones (SEZ) in Shenzhen, Zhuhai, Shantou, and Xiamen. These four open cities located in China's southern coastal provinces of Guangdong and Fujian, all at a safe distance away from the nation's capital, were selected for a new experiment that was aimed to bring in much-needed foreign capitals, ideas, and technologies to China through the narrow gates. In 1984, Beijing designated fourteen additional coastal cities as the Economic and Technological Development Zones. Among them were Beihai and Guangzhou in the south, Shanghai in central China, and Tianjin and Dalian in the north.

1985 to 1991: In the mid-1980s, faced with rising inflation and other problems arising from initial experiments in the market economy, the Chinese government turned to an austerity program. Restrictions were imposed on foreign investment, and the contract value of FDI in 1986 registered a drop of more than 50 percent from the previous year to just under $3 billion. Still more areas were opened for FDI in 1985 (Yangtze River Delta, Pearl River Delta, Minnan River Delta, Liaodong Peninsula, and Jiadong Peninsula), making the entire east China coast a new economic beachhead. Just as China's call for further development of the "Gold Coast" started to spur foreign investment again, the Tiananmen Square crackdown in June 1989 halted FDI. The central government's stricter criteria for FDI approval, which emphasized high technology and export-oriented production, also contributed to a rather flat growth in FDI during this period.

1992 to present: In January 1992, Deng Xiaoping made a grand tour of Guangdong province, during which he personally witnessed and endorsed the progress of economic reforms first introduced to the province twelve years earlier. His reaffirmation of the Open Door Policy gave a fresh boost to China's drive for FDI, leading to Beijing's subsequent announcement to extend the open coastal city status to the country's landlocked region as well. This region stretches from Pudong district in Shanghai ("the dragon's head") to Chongqing ("the dragon's tail"). In 1993, China's total foreign trade reached U.S. $195 billion, accounting for almost 40 percent of its GDP. It is significant to note that nearly 35 percent of that trade was conducted by more than 165,000 foreign-funded enterprises (FFE), then registered at China's Ministry of Foreign Trade and Economic Cooperation. ("China's Foreign Trade in 1993 Over U.S. $195 Billion," 1994)

In the early 1990s, there was a general decline in worldwide foreign investment flows, but foreign capital continued to flow into China. However, alarmed by a dangerously high inflation rate that topped 20 percent in urban areas, Beijing once again introduced the economic retrenchment policy. As a result, in the first decline since the fallout from the Tiananmen Square crackdown, FDI plummeted 50 percent in the first quarter of 1994, compared with the same period a year earlier. The number of newly established FFEs also fell almost 45 percent during the same period. But as the country's economic conditions improved and foreign investors' confidence was restored, FDI inflow climbed to nearly $40 billion in 1995, making China the world's second largest recipient of FDI after the United States.

In the past decade, China has introduced a series of new measures to enhance its location advantages, especially the improvement of pitifully inadequate infrastructure. More roads, more rail, and more power have long been at the top of the agenda for Chinese central and provincial governments. A four-year period from 1991 through 1995 saw the most rapid development in

China's railway construction history, with the country's railways topping 60,000 kilometers. Still, the country is afflicted with serious problems. With demand for electricity outstripping supply, more than 120 million people or one-tenth of the total population live without electricity. Power blackouts continue to plague even the biggest industrial centers, and power shortage is cutting into productivity nationwide. Only now is China determined to build superclass power stations, including its largest transprovincial pool of power companies, the East China Power Network, which will increase its total capacity by more than 50 percent before the year 2000.

Foreign firms are also making greater commitments to accepting opportunities in large infrastructure development projects in China. Britain's Export Credit Guarantee Department, for one, is about to record China as its biggest market for power generation equipment. In spite of a relative lack of location advantages, there is evidence that FDI in China has already entered the growth stage of the development path, as best reflected by the emergence of the consumer market. In the early 1990s, McKinsey and Company estimated that China had some sixty million people with more than U.S. $1,000 annual income—the level at which consumerism begins to blossom. A market research by Hong Kong-based Concord Group claimed that there were then eighty million people with an income of more than U.S. $7,500 a year (Caplen, B., 1992). Even by McKinsey's more conservative estimate, the nation's target consumer population is expected to increase to 200 million by the end of this decade.

China's overall achievement to date in attracting foreign investment is impressive, but the pattern of FDI has been rather skewed. To begin with, there are imbalances in sectors where FDI has been made. An overemphasis on real estate development by foreign investors needs to be redressed; the government's controls must be relaxed to allow investment in other sectors such as telecommunication and transportation in order to upgrade the nation's infrastructure. Moreover, there are imbalances in geographical areas where FDI has been made. With natural advantages, notably their proximity to Hong Kong and Taiwan, China's coastal region has so far attracted 90 percent of the total FDI. Hence, the lack of investment in the inland provinces resulted in gross discrepancies in regional economies.

As early as 1990, the per capita income of Shanghai (approximately U.S. $680) was more than triple that of the national average ($200). The figures for two other leading municipalities, Beijing and Tianjin, were also well ahead of the national average—U.S. $560 and $410, respectively. When the coastal provinces, from Guangdong in the south to Liaoning in the north, were included, the regions boasted the average of about U.S. $380 per capita income. By contrast, the per capita income of the poorest of all, Guizhou province in southwest China, was less than half of the national average. For the nearby landlocked Sichuan, the most populous province in China with more than 100 million people, it was only about U.S. $130 (Child, J., 1994).

To remove such imbalance between regions, Beijing needs to take steps to direct more FDI toward its poorer interior by improving the transport networks and other infrastructures outside the coastal regions as well. Looking ahead, there are three key factors that are likely to shape China's FDI environment:

- Politically, China is now poised at the end of a leadership cycle. Yet, the aging Chinese leaders are unwilling to give up their power, fearing that China may experience political, economic, and social upheavals similar to those seen in the late 1980s in Soviet Union and Eastern Europe.
- Economically, Beijing's policies continue changing in rapid succession. At one time, FDI is highly encouraged. At another time, as the economy becomes overheated, austerity programs are launched. Frequent changes in economic poli-

cies may not contribute positively to China's image as a place to invest.

- In addition, there is growing competition from other developing countries, especially those in Southeast Asia. For example, Vietnam attracted more than 1,000 FDI projects, with a total value of U.S. $10 billion in just six years after 1988, when the country reopened its door to investments from abroad.

In the late 1970s, after thirty years of Communist rule, China was close to bankruptcy—especially during the Cultural Revolution (1966-1976), which severely hurt much of the country's production. For two decades from 1978 to his death in February 1997, Deng had revolutionized China's economic system through the introduction of socialist market economy. Still, his work is left unfinished. The biggest challenge is to transform the country's lackluster state-owned enterprises (SOEs) that today account for almost three-quarters of investment, more than half of total assets, and two-thirds of employment (Foo and Cheung, 1997). Beijing's attempts to reform SOEs have so far been unsuccessful. In 1996, at least half the industrial SOEs incurred net losses equal to 1.3 percent of GDP; the factory capacity utilization rate for key industrial products fell below 60 percent. But SOEs continued to absorb more than three-quarters of domestic credit, thus crowding out investment by nonstate firms—the engines of China's economic growth.

China's FDI policy is still insufficiently transparent, involves excessive levels of government approval, and in many ways is below international standards. As other developing countries continue to improve the FDI climate, China's attractiveness as a recipient country may suffer. To cope with these problems and challenges, Beijing has introduced a number of investor-friendly policies. They include the gradual opening of the domestic market through the relaxation of export ratios for products made by

FFEs and the easing of restrictions on investment in the tertiary sector. The country's retail sector, for one, has already undergone three stages of reform: (1) in 1978, the state monopoly over distribution was dismantled; (2) within six years, price controls were relaxed and the market, rather than the state, began to set prices; and (3) by 1992, the mandatory purchase and sale through state-owned wholesalers was abolished, and manufacturers were allowed to choose their own buyers or operate their own outlets.

The bold reform thus carried out by Beijing attracted several Japanese retailers. Yaohan became the first foreign firm to obtain the official approval to get directly involved in a large-scale retailing business in China. It opened a joint venture department store in Beijing in 1992 and a supermarket in Shanghai two years later. The company plans to build a network of chain stores throughout China, with a target of 1,000 supermarkets and 3,000 fast-food restaurants by the year 2010. In 1996, Daiei, Japan's largest retailer and operator of the convenience store chain, Lawson ("the 7-Eleven of Japan"), also announced a plan to set up 100 new stores a year in major Chinese cities, beginning with the opening of its store in Shanghai.

STRATEGIES FOR CHINA BUSINESS

In 1949, the Communists emerged victorious from the Chinese Civil War (1945-1949). Japan, being a close political ally to the United States in the Far East, did not recognize the People's Republic of China (PRC) as the legal government of China, and Tokyo remained hostile toward PRC for nearly two decades. However, toward the end of the 1960s, when the Cultural Revolution was still raging throughout China, the Japanese attitude toward China began to change. The attitude was prompted by a pragmatic assessment of the changing international situation, prospects of closer economic ties with China, and old cultural bonds. Then, in July 1971, U.S. President Richard Nixon announced a dramatic change in Sino-American relations by revealing Foreign Affairs Advisor Dr. Henry Kissinger's secret trip to Beijing and his own acceptance of an invitation to visit PRC in the following year.

This move by the United States was a great surprise to the international community, especially to a Japan that had been precluded by the United States from developing closer ties with China. The Japanese felt that the lack of prior consultation concerning such an important decision was inappropriate and rather insulting. Prior to Nixon's announcement, which mollified twenty-two years of hostility toward China, Tokyo had intended to gradually improve its own relations with Beijing; the "Nixon Shock" provided Japan the impetus to expedite the process. At about the same time, the Chinese attitude toward Japan also changed dramatically; they no longer attacked Japanese economic imperialism. A series of these events paved the way for Japanese Premier Kakuei Tanaka's visit to Beijing in September 1972. His visit quickly produced an agreement to establish full diplomatic relations between the two countries, nearly seven years ahead of the signing of a similar Sino-American agreement.

The normalization of Sino-Japanese relations signaled a greater role for Japan's investment and technical assistance in China's economic development; Japanese firms' advance into China began soon afterward. Nonetheless, their China business strategies since could only be characterized by a cautious, step-by-step approach:

- Step 1: *"Selling to China"* (Early 1970s—Mid-1980s)
  Japanese firms remained extremely prudent about committing their capital, with a majority simply concentrating on the export of finished products from Japan. However, the actual progress of making inroads into China was rather slow due to the very low purchasing power of consumers.

- Step 2: *"Manufacturing in China"* (Mid-1980s—Late-1980s)

  Following the signing of the Plaza Accord in 1985, there commenced a general boom of FDI in Asia, and China made full use of this opportunity. Hence, the strategy started to shift from selling to China to manufacturing in China. The signing of the Sino-Japanese Bilateral Investment Treaty in 1988 further induced Japanese firms to place a greater emphasis on manufacturing through FDI.

- Step 3: *"Manufacturing and Selling in China"* (Early 1990s—Present)

  At the beginning of the 1990s, encouraged by the emergence of consumer markets in China, Japanese firms started eyeing the country's domestic market. Accordingly, the strategy shifted to manufacturing and selling in China. At present, more than 30 percent of Japanese factories in China are still oriented toward the Japanese market. However, this is expected to drop to below 20 percent in 1997, leaving 70 percent of the factories to serve the Chinese market.

The cautious approach to China business adopted by Japanese firms may reflect their general tendency to "play it safe" in little-known parts of the business. Japanese managers generally exhibit a much higher level of uncertainty avoidance than their Western counterparts (Hofstede, 1980). Also, the extreme caution concerning investment in China illustrates their risk-averse nature. Moreover, the way the Japanese perceive and react to risks is also different from that of Americans and Europeans. The 1989 Tiananmen Square crackdown was a risk crisis to all foreign investors. In its aftermath, many Western firms pulled back or scaled down their operations in China. However, most Japanese firms just carried on, perceiving the incident simply as a short-term change of risk situations in China. Their business strategies remained sharply focused on long-term gains in the market share relative to their competitors. This is in contrast to the Western firms' preoccupation with rather short-term returns on investments as measured by current earnings and stock prices.

Before moving into a new market, Japanese firms often let competitors test the water first, and wait patiently for the infrastructure to improve and the market to mature. All the while, they keep their eyes on the problems encountered and progresses made by others to learn as many lessons as possible from others' experiences. Japanese firms are also known to make drastic moves when heavy pressure is applied upon them by the host-country government and, especially, by their competitors. This is a reflection of the single overriding characteristic of Japanese firms, that is, the unrelenting focus on competitive position. In other words, they pay close attention to competitive reactions to changes in product, pricing, distribution methods, and so on, or to the possibility that competitors may see different patterns and opportunities in different parts of business (Abegglen and Stalk, 1985).

In the mid-1980s, several Western carmakers plunged head-long into China. In January 1984, Beijing Jeep, 31 percent owned by Chrysler of the United States, became China's first joint venture carmaker. By January 1996, it had produced more than half a million cars worth nearly U.S. $3 billion. Shanghai Volkswagen, a 50/50 joint venture formally agreed upon in October 1984 by Volkswagen (VW) of Germany and three Chinese parties, has also been operating in China for more than ten years. By the end of February 1997, it sold more than one million cars in China. Then, in 1995, Daimler-Benz of Germany won approval to build a $1 billion multipurpose vehicle factory in Guangdong province with two Chinese partners. In the same year, General Motors (GM) also signed a $1 billion joint venture agreement to become the first American carmaker to set up sedan vehicle production facilities in China. GM's 50/50 joint venture with Shanghai Automotive (China's biggest carmaker and VW's local partner for Shanghai Volkswagen) plans to build a factory with an annual production capacity of 100,000 cars.

By contrast, Japanese carmakers long remained wary of direct investment in China, and apart from three relatively small carmakers (Daihatsu, Isuzu, and Suzuki), they have hardly charged into China. They preferred exporting finished products to building factories, and a result, they soon became China's leading source of car imports. In 1994, Honda Motor actually reached an agreement to set up a 50/50 joint venture in Guangzhou to assemble Civic Sedans, but the project never got off the ground due to signs that the Chinese government was planning to tighten restrictions on car assembly projects involving foreigners.

Toyota Motor had negotiated with the Chinese government for over a decade, trying to modify investment terms that it believed made no commercial sense. Beijing wanted more than a factory, pressing Toyota to build a community with schools, hospitals, and roads. Then, there was a constant tug-of-war over technology transfer. China wanted the Japanese to enter joint ventures in which they had less than 50 percent control but 100 percent willingness to transfer technology. The Chinese asked for state-of-the-art equipment for assembly, but Toyota insisted that the level of China's auto parts industry was too low to support the use of its advanced equipment. Furthermore, Japanese managers doubted whether Chinese workers could muster the assembly line discipline required of them under the advanced mass production system.

In spite of such wariness, Japanese carmakers have been steadily moving ahead to capitalize on China's fast-growing market, where about 1.6 million cars, trucks, and other vehicles were sold in 1996. Honda, for one, has established successful joint ventures netting almost 20 percent of the world's largest motorcycle market of more than three million units a year. Honda believes that soaring individual incomes will continue to increase demand for motorcycles through the rest of this century. Though the company failed to begin a car assembly project earlier, it has a plan for a $20 million joint venture to build an auto parts factory in Guangdong province.

Some firms found an anchor for their China business expansion even without getting their feet very wet. In August 1995, Isuzu Motor became the first foreign firm to take control of a Chinese carmaker through the transfer of legal persons' shares, which were owned by government bodies and institutions and thus could not be traded on stock exchanges. With only a 15 percent stake in Beijing Light Bus, the company put the minibus maker under its control with the appointment of the chief of Isuzu's quality assurance as the general manager. Then, in the spring of 1996, after years of hard negotiations, Toyota finally obtained an official approval from Beijing for its U.S. $165 million joint venture agreement with Tianjin Automotive to produce car engines. Together they will build 1300cc engines for use in China and other Asian countries at an annual rate of 100,000 units.

As the Chinese government continues to cultivate more investor-friendly environments, the country's location advantages for FDI should grow further. Moreover, as the country's enterprises accumulate modern technology and know-how, the ownership advantages for FDI should also rise. The Japanese see that China is no longer a market of the future but the one warranting top-level actions today. Needless to say, there are still many hurdles to be cleared. The sources of obstacles are not just political and economic barriers; many firms operating in China are also facing barriers of peculiar and traditional business customs in the personal network society of China. To overcome these barriers, Japanese firms are increasingly resorting to strategic alliances with Chinese partners.

Chapter 3

China—Catching Up on Lost Time

- More than 2,200 years ago, Ch'in Shihuang ("the first Emperor of China") laid down the foundation of China's management tradition; however, the upgrading of management knowledge and techniques remains as the task of utmost importance for China today.
- After the death of Mao Zedong in 1976, Deng Xiaoping introduced a series of bold measures for management reforms to revitalize and modernize Chinese enterprises.
- China has turned to the West for help in management training and development; in recent years, it has also started to turn to its ancient military strategies for their application to modern management.

CHINA'S MANAGEMENT TRADITION

China is the nation that boasts more than 4,000 years of continuous civilization. It also has the world's oldest bureaucracy that has survived for more than twenty centuries. In 221 B.C., Ch'in Shihuang, "the first Emperor of China," founded a dynasty that unified the country and gave China its present name in Western language. He centralized political authority and ran the empire by dividing it into thirty-six commanderies. Each commandery was under the authority of a civil administrator and a military governor. Appointed by and made responsible to the central government, these two officials worked under the watchful eyes of an overseer. This centrally organized bureaucracy was to become the basis of the imperial system in China until the turn of this century.

The Emperor was a tyrannical ruler and did not hesitate to use severe punishments to deal with the opposition, but he was a man of exceptional vision and capability. Today he is perhaps best remembered as the man who embarked on a complex construction project of grand scale—the Great Wall of China. During a short eleven-year reign, he also conducted a census and standardized the written language, laws, coinage, weights, and measures. Xian, the capital of Ch'in dynasty, was the starting point of the famed Silk Road. Along that road, traders of ancient times carried with them not only much-prized goods but also the advanced knowledge that China then had to offer to the West. Looking at the many imprints that he left on the development of China as a nation, we can only conclude that "the first Emperor of China" was indeed a great manager of his era.

The Emperor's military strategies and much of his thinking on management mirrored the doctrines of Sun Tzu, who had authored the oldest military classic known in Chinese literature—*The Art of War* (Wee, Lee, and Bambang, 1991). In this 2,300-year-old classic, Sun Tzu advocated that the pinnacle of strategic attainment was to win without even fighting. The sage of ancient China said that warfare and confrontation was not the first option to be pursued. Nevertheless, he provided several important principles in case one had to resort to arms. The "Principle of Simplicity" suggests that successful strategies are often deceptively simple so that their wisdom is not even noticed. Though this principle argues for direct and simple plans that can be easily understood and implemented by soldiers and officers, it does not contradict the need for detailed planning by generals.

A war involves more than one party, each pursuing different and varied strategies depending on the prevailing conditions; as it is impossible to predict with certainty the enemy's strategies, battle plans should not be rigid. Sun Tzu's "Principle of Adaptability" contends that alternative plans must be formulated in anticipation of the changing patterns of war. He explained this principle by comparing battle plans to water—just as water shapes itself according to the ground, battle plans should be formulated in accordance with the situation of the enemy; as water has no constant shape, in warfare there are no fixed rules and conditions; and just as flowing water avoids the heights and hastens to the lowlands, battle plans must be drawn to avoid the strengths and strike the weaknesses of the enemy.

In formulating battle plans, one must have information about the enemy as well as weather and terrain. Calling it foreknowledge, Sun Tzu said that the enlightened ruler and the wise general could not achieve victories over the enemies unless they had fore-knowledge, and it could only be obtained from people who were familiar with the enemy; without such people on your side, superior weapons and plans per se could not win wars. He thus argued that a ruler must have moral influence on people to enable them to be in perfect accord with their ruler, for whom they willingly face life and death without fear for danger; the general must hold qualities of wisdom, sincerity, benevolence, courage, and strictness.

For the actual implementation of battle plans, Sun Tzu provided the "Principle of Deception." According to him, warfare is based on deception—when capable, pretend incapability; when active, pretend inactivity; when near, make it appear you are far away; and so on. The purpose of deception is to mislead and surprise the enemy and to capitalize on his unpreparedness, thereby increasing your own chance of winning. Sun Tzu's military strategies are known to have been used extensively by generations of rulers in China. In essence, he explained the principles of the execution of war strategies as follows (Wee, Lee, and Bambang, 1991, p. 3):

In movement, be as swift as the *wind*;
In slow march, be as majestic as the *forest*;

In raid, be as fierce as *fire*;
In defense, be as firm as *mountains*;
In camouflage, be as impenetrable as *darkness*;
When striking, be as overwhelming as *thunderbolts.*

Many Japanese military writings also bear influence from Sun Tzu's work. For example, Miyamoto Musashi's *Book of Five Rings* ("Gorin no Sho"), a military classic written circa 1645 A.D., contains many parallels to Sun Tzu's works, including the five elements of earth, water, fire, wind, and void (Brown et al., 1982). In modern warfare, his book is said to have influenced Japanese military strategies and their conduct of war. Moreover, Musashi's military thinking and strategies have had tremendous influence on Japanese management. In business or military warfare, the ultimate aim is to win. Competition in business can be as vicious and ruthless as on the battleground. Managers and workers field the business arena, just as the battleground is fielded by generals and soldiers. Businesses have collapsed because of incompetent leaders, ill-chosen strategies, poor information gathering and planning, mismanagement of human and other resources, and inability to outsmart competitors; this is no different from war. In fact, during the 1970s and early 1980s, *The Book of Five Rings* was reputedly a "must" book for Japanese executives.

During the Sino-Japanese War (1937-1945) and the Chinese Civil War (1945-1949), Mao Zedong used many of Sun Tzu's strategies masterfully to rout the external enemy, the Japanese, and then the internal enemy, the Nationalists led by Chiang Kai-shek. Mao thus completed the Communist conquest of mainland China to establish the People's Republic of China on October 1, 1949. Although the Japanese borrowed and effectively applied China's ancient military thinking to both military and business warfare in the modern era, it does not seem that the influence of Sun Tzu in China extended beyond the military philosophy of Mao Zedong, stopping short of influencing the management of business under Mao's reign. In fact, one of the major concerns of Chinese leaders today is the upgrading of management knowledge and techniques.

GLIMPSE OF CHINESE MANAGEMENT TODAY

In a socialist country such as China, it is extremely difficult to find out exactly what the prevailing management practices are. However, even a small collection of cases, gathered over the past fifteen years on my visits to China, may be useful for obtaining a glimpse of contemporary Chinese management.

Case 1: An Engineer's Dilemma

In 1981 when I was invited to hold management seminars, a young engineer working at a state-owned factory with over 15,000 workers paid me a visit. Two years earlier, the factory management decided to automate the entire pipe fabricating process through the use of a computer-based system. However, their planned purchase of a turnkey system from a major U.S. computer manufacturer fell through, due to unique and stringent requirements imposed by the factory. Subsequently, each of the five departments involved in the total process was authorized to select and order its own equipment.

The engineer confessed, "The new automated process developed by five departments appeared to work very nicely on paper. But it was done without much consultation and thought on the interface problem, and we soon found ourselves in the pit." He continued, "The factory has already purchased the central control processor, which is supposed to coordinate the work of all the equipment to be used. Yet, nobody really knows how to make it work. Worst of all, I have just been given the job of cleaning up this mess." Seeing him trapped in such an impossible situation, I suggested that he should perhaps start looking for a job elsewhere.

However, in a society where the rejection of a job assigned by higher authorities could easily lead to a less desirable job or even dismissal, this was much easier said than done. This case illustrates a lack of well-thought plans on the part of management. Planning implies not only the introduction of new ideas and things but also sensible and workable innovations. Having failed to follow this basic principle of management, it is not at all surprising that the work to automate the factory came to a grinding halt shortly afterward, at considerable costs. A few years later, this engineer managed to relocate himself and his family to the United States, where he now works for an American company.

Case 2: Shortage of Qualified Staff

In the early 1980s when I first visited a prestigious research institute, its computer center was equipped with an outdated, second-generation main computer and a couple of microcomputers. However, soon afterward, benefiting from the central government's ambitious drive for modernization in science and technology, the facilities were upgraded through the installation of an up-to-date main computer along with nearly twenty personal computers of various makes and models. The institute even began to use personal computers to run computerized business and management information systems. However, the fruit of their efforts appeared minimal.

The deputy director of the institute admitted, "We are very short of qualified staff, particularly in commercial applications areas. That woman over there, for example, must look after the development of new application software as well as the maintenance of hardware and systems software. Her section has already computerized payroll and accounting systems, but they have a long way to go before integrating all these and other application systems now in the pipeline into a total management information system." As such, most of the newly acquired personal computers were standing idle.

Due to acute shortage of experienced staff, the clear assignment of organizational activities and delegation of authorities, though considered absolutely necessary by the institute's management, was far from actual reality. In order to lessen the problem, the institute sent senior research associates abroad to study modern computer technology and management. However, as recently as the mid-1980s, it was still in the process of phasing out redundant staff, revamping the organizational structure, instituting the merit-based performance appraisal system, and introducing several other measures to boost staff productivity and morale.

Case 3: Mediocre Services

After several visits to a thriving industrial city in southwest China, I became a regular customer at a rather somber-looking, four-star hotel built in 1962 by Russians. The hotel's main restaurant was acclaimed as the place to taste some of the region's best specialty dishes. The food they served was excellent, but I was totally dismayed by the poor service. Diners were often seen unattended with dirty dishes still on the table. Some chose to clear up the table themselves, when their efforts to get the attention of restaurant staff had all but failed. To make matters worse, there was nobody in sight who could be recognized as the person in charge. "Why on earth are you giving us such poor service?" I asked. The answer given by one waitress to this simple question was most revealing, and I soon began to see the underlying problems.

"To begin with, I don't particularly like this job," she replied. After graduating from a secondary school, the girl wanted to work as an interpreter or a tour guide. However, after taking the government-administered test, she was assigned to the hotel job against her personal wishes. Besides the job's limited career opportunities, she resented the long working hours which stretched from 6:30 in the morning to 9:30 in the evening. She actually worked nine hours a day, with a short break between meals, and received one day off every five days. She was provided with meals and a dormitory room at the hotel where she could sleep overnight. This seemingly comfortable arrangement was, in reality, not received very favorably by her and other young workers, who were mostly in their late teens and early twenties.

Transferring her anger at the job to the management, she said, "Our management refuses to accept even the existence of problems." This statement was rather odd in view of the fact that a guest opinion card was placed on every table. I soon learned that most customers did not bother to fill out the card, and the absence of feedback was conveniently interpreted by the management as an indication of satisfactory services. I was also told that by purposely working slowly and offering only mediocre services, restaurant staff were secretly hoping that their customers would file complaints to alert management to the problems. In short, management was failing to meet customers' needs, supervise staff's work, and recognize deeply rooted resentment among the staff.

Case 4: Frustrated Travelers

Due to language barriers and bureaucratic red tape in China, a great majority of tourists from abroad have no choice but to rely on the state-run travel bureau. The bureau offers services ranging from securing visas and booking reservations with airlines and hotels to determining where and what to eat in China, at hefty fees. One naturally expects that a tour prearranged by them will go smoothly. Yet, as more and more Chinese cities and towns are opened to foreign tourists, an increasing number of complaints are heard about the services actually rendered in China. Not so long ago, my own adventure turned into a nightmare. Knowing that booking reservations on China's domestic flights must be done at least one week beforehand, I visited the bureau's branch office in Chengdu to plan ahead for a trip from Xian (my next destination) to Hong Kong (the final destination). The conversation between a travel agent and me went something like this:

> "Are there any flights from Xian to Hong Kong next Monday?"
>
> "Yes, I think so."
>
> "That's great! Can you get me a ticket for an afternoon flight?"
>
> "No, I cannot do it here. Since you will be taking off from Xian, you must buy the ticket there."
>
> "Well, can't you at least give them a call to reserve a seat for me?"
>
> "Sorry, it's our policy not to take any reservation over the phone. You must go to our Xian office, okay?"
>
> "But . . ."

I could not get any further with this agent, who appeared more eager to get rid of me than to offer help. Four days later, immediately on reaching Xian, I rushed over to the bureau's office. This visit again turned out to be futile and frustrating. I was simply told, "All flights to Hong Kong are booked solid for the next five days." In the end, I somehow managed to buy a railway ticket for a rough three-day trip back to Hong Kong. This case illustrates a total lack of provisions to coordinate activities based on the efficient flow of information horizontally and vertically within an organization.

The four cases above may serve to show problems of different kinds and degrees related to the process of management. The first case, "An Engineer's Dilemma," describes a problem arising largely from failure to perform the most basic function of management—planning. "Shortage of Qualified Staff" presents a serious problem in organizing and staffing that led to the poor utilization of technologies, especially software. The last two cases drawn from service organizations highlight a lack of effective management in directing and controlling. Here, we are also struck with the impression that a simple marketing concept such as "Consumers are King" is almost completely absent. The absence of the concept may be explained by the economic, political-legal, and social-cultural environments in China, which are obviously quite different from those generally found in the West.

DENG XIAOPING'S MANAGEMENT REFORM

In the last fifty years, China's economic and political systems have gone through notable changes, especially after the death of Mao Zedong in 1976 and the subsequent ascent of Deng Xiaoping as the undisputed leader of China. Mao, who often compared himself to Emperor Ch'in Shihuang, followed the doctrine of legalism and ruled the country through tight control by the central government. However, his successor Deng adopted more of a Confucian doctrine and gave a greater degree of autonomy to local governments and enterprises. By the early 1990s, the revitalization of state-owned enterprises (SOEs) became a top priority for the Chinese leadership.

In 1992, Beijing formally promulgated "Regulations for Transforming Managerial Mechanisms of the State-Owned Enterprises." Some served to clarify ambiguities in the existing regulations, but the majority of them were aimed at giving SOEs much-expanded power, most notably in human resource management, production management, pricing decisions, import/export decisions, and investment decisions (Chen, 1995). Accordingly, SOEs were allowed to decide whom, when, and how to hire and reward their own employees. They were also given the rights to make and adjust their production commitment, freely set prices for their products, participate in trade negotiations with foreign businesses, and invest their reserve capital in China as well as abroad.

Moreover, to curve administrative intervention, the new regulations also stipulated that government institutions would face legal consequences for trespassing on the autonomy of SOEs. In effect, the regulations made the government responsible mainly for creating conditions conducive to transforming SOEs' management through the promotion of a market economy. The government was also made responsible for reducing SOEs' financial burden through the establishment of a comprehensive social security system and the development of public facilities and welfare institutions.

In more recent years, however, as China took unprecedented steps toward management reform, many taboos were lifted. The central government announced that it would cut bank funds and power supplies to inefficient SOEs; foreign firms were allowed to buy controlling interest in SOEs; as part of a plan for the nationwide housing reform, private citizens were allowed to buy their own properties. Beijing also revealed plans to replace free health care covering 130 million people with a system funded by the state, enterprises, and workers. In spite of all these changes, the lack of strong economic incentives for individuals still haunts China today, and it has led to the appearance of new kinds of work ethics among highly motivated individuals.

People working for an SOE generally receive nearly the same salary or wage, no matter how long and hard they work. As a result, many have resorted to putting as little time as possible into their regular work, so that they can spend more of their time and energy on starting and running their own private businesses. The five-days-a-week work program recently introduced by many enterprises to alleviate their chronic overstaffing problem is further encouraging the birth of a new breed of entrepreneurs, often at the expense of their employers. Needless to say, there are many who devote themselves to work at regular jobs. To them, which organization or work unit they belong to is still very important because of the social status, privileges, and other intangible benefits that come with the job they hold.

Senior executives, for one, stay loyal to their employers, with little or no time to run private businesses on the side. However, it is not uncommon to spot people showing up for work only a day or two every week, doing almost nothing but drinking tea, reading newspapers, or chatting. In a work environment such as this, one might conclude that an SOE is a great place for the mediocre as well as the very ambitious. I was surprised to learn that an increasing number of enterprising individuals were taking a long leave of absence, without pay, to try their luck in moneymaking ventures outside their regular jobs. And to ensure that they have a job to go back to, in case the venture fails, some are even paying their employer part of their regular monthly pay during the leave period!

Although the behavior of people at work is necessarily influenced by the environment surrounding an organization, it is more directly affected by the management. Management is not only a process but also a philosophy. This philosophy may be broadly defined in terms of the management's attitudes toward employees, consumers, suppliers, owners, and society. It must be learned and accepted by a majority of people before it can actually be applied to the practice of management. China has been shaping a new philosophy of management since it opened its door to the outside world twenty years ago. Still, to many Chinese organizations, management is a little-known concept. The education level of people has a great impact on the quality of managers and workers. China's central government believes that the promotion of education is a prerequisite for management reforms.

Prior to the establishment of the People's Republic of China (PRC) in 1949, only about 20 percent of school-age children were enrolled in primary school. More than 80 percent of the whole population was illiterate, while in the rural areas the illiteracy rate was over 95 percent. One of the first and most important tasks of the government was to provide primary education for as many children as possible. The Cultural Revolution created ten years of stagnation at all levels of education in China. Still, by the time Mao Zedong passed away, 96 percent of the nation's school-age children were attending primary school. After economic reform was launched in 1978, the government also started to invest very heavily in higher education.

Students' enrollment in secondary technical schools rose from 890,000 in 1978 to more than 1.5 million in 1985. Similarly, enrollment in colleges and universities doubled from 860,000 to just over 1.7 million during the same period. Many of the nation's major universities formally introduced management courses at both undergraduate and graduate levels. For example, in Shenzhen—a booming Special Economic Zone, right across the border from Hong Kong—a brand-new university was established to produce American-style MBA graduates equipped with modern management knowledge and skills. Today, besides these educational institutions, training centers set up by foreign nationals are running programs for Chinese managers all over the country: Sino-American National Center for Industrial Science and Technology (Dalian), Sino-Japanese Enterprise Center (Tianjin), Sino-Canada Enterprise Management Training Center (Chengdu), and Sino-German Industrial Management Training Center (Shanghai).

Although management reform has not quite taken root in China, considerable changes have occurred since the heady days of the Cultural Revolution, as far as managers are concerned. There have been attempts to investigate the behavior of Chinese managers relative to managers in the West. However, many of those studies were conducted by people unfamiliar with China, and they failed to produce a valid and reliable description of Chinese management behavior. A study conducted in the late 1980s, for example, noted a great degree of age-related difference; older managers who experienced the Cultural Revolution were found to hold considerably more conservative views than their younger colleagues who did not live through the same experience (Adler and Campbell, 1989). Over a period of thirty years, from the founding of PRC in 1949 to the beginning of its current management reform in 1979, China went through three major stages of management development:

- *Stage 1:* Soon after the Communists' victory over the Nationalists, state ownership of enterprises and the Soviet model of management were introduced to China. Executive authority in SOEs was concentrated in the hands of technically trained directors—the so-called "One Director Management System." Throughout the 1950s, this system made considerable contributions to heavy industrial development in China.
- *Stage 2:* The bureaucratic top-down management imported from the Soviets did not fit very well with the Chinese communists' aspirations of greater roles for Party officials and workers. And as Moscow-Beijing Axis deteriorated rapidly toward the end of the 1950s, the Soviet model was weakened; factory directors were placed under the leadership of Party committees and became only responsible for the implementation of decisions made by those committees.
- *Stage 3:* The new management system with Chinese characteristics was disrupted by the Cultural Revolution, in which managers were discredited while the representatives of revolutionary workers were given power to run enterprises, subject to the guidance of ideologically loyal Party committees.

Though the style of management in China has moved away from the original Soviet-style model, it still exhibits a high degree of the concentration of authority; decision-making powers are centralized within the enterprise or retained by higher authorities. However, the models are different in terms of the structuring of organizational activities. The Soviet model represented the explicit structuring of activities, whereby work and responsibilities in organizations were formally laid down according to standard procedures and allocated to designated specialties. On the other hand, China's SOE today may be termed as an "implicitly structured organization"; the structuring of activities is imprecise in terms of procedures, definitions of responsibility, and so on (Child, 1994).

The ongoing economic reform is seeking to decentralize authority and define managerial responsibilities more clearly. Its intention is to encourage enterprises to enter into a wider range of market transactions, which they will search out and then negotiate for on their own initiative. In 1984, after five years of bold experiments in the market economy in Sichuan province (the birthplace of Deng Xiaoping), the Communist Party Central Committee launched the Enterprise Responsibility System. It was designed to enhance the autonomy and responsibility of enterprises through various types of contracts with higher authorities.

Starting in 1985, all SOEs were required to implement the new system under the leadership of the enterprise director, replacing the old system run under the leadership of the Party committee. Thus, the director was once again placed at the apex of the enterprise and represented the highest decision maker. Within the enterprise, the Director Responsibility System is being used to identify and structure the executive powers of management. In short, the current economic reform is intended to move Chinese management away from operating under externally imposed norms toward working under internally generated norms. However, the gap between the vision of a modern industrial society and the present reality in China is still substantial.

The shortage of managerial and professional expertise constrains the decentralization of authority and delegation of decision making within the enterprise. Moreover, the limited communication and information infrastructures constrain the diffusion of information that would otherwise assist enterprise managers in taking initiatives in the market. The expectation is that China will continue its learning process, through which the dynamic for improvement will come from the actions of managers and workers rather than from directives passed down from above. It is vital that all those involved in this process keep an open mind and stay well informed about the Western concepts and practices of modern management. However, China's top leaders have repeatedly stated that China should not absorb everything from others. Hence, they are turning to their own military classics for application to management.

Over several millennia of practicing and refining techniques, Chinese military strategists learned that the highest principle of all was flexibility. In *The Art of War*, Sun Tzu pointed out the value of flexibility by comparing adaptability in warfare to the behavior of water. The doctrine of Lao Tzu also noted that water was at once the most yielding of elements and the mightiest of eroding forces (Blakney, 1980). Another Chinese classic, *The Book of Changes* ("*I Ching*"), expounded the philosophy of the unity of opposites as the notion of *yin* and *yang* (Siu, 1968). *Yin* is the female element, manifested in earth, wind, and water and associated with darkness and enclosure; *yang*, the male element, is manifested in heaven, thunder, fire, and mountains and associated with light and openness. As described earlier in this chapter, both of these elements are also included in Sun Tzu's principle of the execution of war strategies.

The philosophy of unity of opposites, especially *yin,* appears throughout the time-honored *36 Stratagems of Ancient China* (Gao, 1991), which was not authored by a single genius but by generations of military leaders and tacticians, politicians, merchants, philosophers, and poets. The ancient Chinese considered schemes and stratagems, often planned and implemented in secrecy, to belong to *yin.* Among the thirty-six stratagems are:

1. make a feint to the east while attacking the west,
2. pretend to take one path while sneaking down another,

3. befriend a distant state while attacking the neighbor,
4. play dumb while remaining smart, and
5. inflict injury on oneself to win the enemy's trust.

The world has gone through vast changes since the days of these Chinese sagas. After opening up to the world in the late 1970s, the Chinese turned to the outside world for much- needed help in management training and development. In recent years, they started turning to their own classics as well. Still, the fruit of their efforts appears rather limited. Today, China is a country in dire need of management reform. Its current drive to learn and adopt some of the West's modern management knowledge and techniques, coupled with serious efforts to reexamine its own ancient military strategies and relate their application to modern management, could well be a clear sign of China catching up on lost time.

Chapter 4

Managing China Business

- Foreign firms may not necessarily change their fundamental strategies or visions simply to adjust to China's mythical elements of market, but they must be aware that China is still a tough place to make money.
- The principal sources of problems that foreign investors have encountered so far in China are managerial barriers, and the management of people poses the greatest challenge to all engaged in China business.
- The natural evolution of management compounds difficulties in determining the transferability of Japanese-style management to China, but bold experiments are being carried out by Japanese firms, small and large.

LAND OF MANY PROMISES

Soon after opening up to the world in 1978, China offered foreign investors a promise of unspecified profits, at an indeterminate future date, in return for their capital and technology. That was, and still is, the country's economic bargain with the outside world. There was then a general perception that anything foreign would sell, and there was plenty of room for all foreign firms in China. In the early 1980s, China was indeed the sellers' market for many foreign products, and many rushed to the land of promise in search of a 1.2 billion-strong consumer market. However, most of them did not find it. By the late 1980s, as competition became keen, China turned into the buyers' market.

Today, with its economic reform in high gear, the country is no doubt one of the world's most attractive investment opportunities, and its once mythical market is increasingly becoming a reality. Still, for foreign investors, China is a tough place to make money. For one thing, only a small proportion of the country's huge population can afford to buy foreign products. More than 70 percent of Chinese live in rural areas and survive on about U.S. $10 a month or less. In interior China, the average monthly wage paid by state-owned enterprises (SOEs) amounts to less than $40. In China's booming coastal regions, where most foreign-funded enterprises (FFEs) operate, the average income is much higher. For example, in Shenzhen Special Economic Zone near Hong Kong, factory workers typically receive $100 per month, but this represents only about one-tenth of that paid in Hong Kong.

Besides people's limited purchasing power, FFEs discovered that overall operational costs were not as low as originally anticipated. When they sought to procure raw materials locally, they often found that SOEs had priority, prices varied each time an order was placed, quality was poor, and promised delivery dates were not always met. A majority of them also experienced difficulties in getting customers to pay bills. As a result, many ended up with lower profit margins in China than in other more mature markets. Nonetheless, a 1995 study carried out by Anderson Consulting and the Economist Intelligence Unit showed that nearly 65 percent of more than 200 multinationals surveyed were making money in China (Clayton, 1995).

The study noted that the most important factors impacting profitability were human resource, cost control, and product quality; these were business basics that could be managed by multinationals anywhere in the world. With the emergence of practices largely modeled after modern Western management, Chinese are also beginning to understand these business basics and other managerial premises inherent in the market economy.

However, much of China's management system is inherited from traditional SOEs, and actual implementation is more often than not difficult. For example, there is one notion that is still deeply ingrained in the minds of Chinese—"Three Iron Rice Bowls": (1) state subsidy for losses incurred by enterprises, (2) permanent job security for employees, and (3) cradle-to-grave welfare for employees' families.

In the mid-1990s, I visited an SOE in China's southwestern hinterland. The company, with annual production of about 2,000 buses, was the leading bus maker in the province, where it boasted a 40 percent market share. However, its sales were sagging and factories were operating only at half capacity; the dismissal or reassignment of workers was next to impossible due to pressure put on the management by trade unions and government officials. The plant manager lamented that overstaffing was a perennial problem. Moreover, the company had to provide not only its employees but also their families with housing, schooling, medical and dental, and a host of other benefits, even after they retired from active work.

Coupled with these operational and financial problems arising largely from the inherited practices, the company was also having a serious problem with employees' low productivity, poor attitudes, nonobservance of rules and regulations, and failure to report problems to the management. The plant manager attributed the problem to the Cultural Revolution that had had destructive impacts on employees' work motivation. In fact, the nationwide turmoil had detrimental effects on China's entire human resource system. For ten years from 1966 to 1976, higher education was practically suspended, and a whole generation of well-educated managers is in effect missing.

Several studies on work motivation conducted in Hong Kong (Fukuda, 1988) have revealed that financial reward is considered one of the most important motivating factors for Chinese workers in Hong Kong. The Chinese generally have a high expectation that any personal achievement must be first met with monetary reward. This pattern is consistent with the postindustrialization hypothesis, which suggests that in developing or newly industrialized countries, materialistic values are highly endorsed. The studies have also indicated that:

- Job-related factors such as challenging work and opportunities for promotion are considered by the Chinese as the most important motivating factor.
- Interpersonal attributes are somewhat important.
- Company-related factors such as job security, benefits, and working conditions are least important.

In order to determine whether or not a similar pattern could be found in mainland China, we conducted a questionnaire survey of fifty workers in the city where the bus assembly company was located. The survey respondents, almost equally distributed by gender, were drawn from three SOEs engaged in manufacturing or trading. The duration of their employment ranged from four to forty-six years, with an average of twenty-three. When asked to rank the factors of motivation according to their importance, they responded with a ranking order rather similar to that reported by the Hong Kong studies—(1) job itself, (2) pay, (3) boss, (4) colleagues, (5) company, and (6) promotion.

Nevertheless, mainland Chinese were different from Hong Kong Chinese in two aspects. First, although considering such company-related factors as "job security" unimportant, the mainlanders regarded "benefits" provided by the company as important as pay. Second, whereas "challenging work" was regarded as the most important motivating factor, another job-related factor, "opportunities for promotion," was considered least important. The discrepancy thus found between the two groups of Chinese could be explained partly by the notion of "Iron Rice Bowls" still prevalent in China. For one, mainlanders turned out to be different from Hong Kong Chinese in that they felt they had very little control over the outcome of their own personal efforts.

A serious search for new theoretical foundations of work motivation began in the West only in the early 1960s. Maslow's Need Hierarchy Theory (1943), Herzberg's Two-Factor Theory (1966), and Vroom's Expectancy Theory (1964), to name a few, have been developed since. However, several studies have presented evidence that the concepts and techniques of motivation developed in the Western context are culture specific, and their use may even be detrimental to organizational effectiveness in other cultures (Hofstcde, 1980). As noted above, even in culturally similar societies such as Hong Kong and mainland China, the universality of the concepts and techniques of work motivation cannot be assumed.

For lack of systematic studies to date, it is not easy to determine how to effectively manage human resources in China. This becomes a real challenge for foreign managers, who know little about the Chinese ways of managing. To circumvent the problem, many foreign firms set up joint ventures with Chinese businesses. However, in reality, the problems of Chinese partners, such as overstaffing and lack of work motivation, are often shiftcd to joint ventures (Li and Tse, 1993).

Under the joint-venture arrangement, Chinesc partners normally supply all local employees, giving little say to foreign partners about their actual choice or pay and benefits. Leaving such important issues to Chinese partners makes it difficult for foreign managers to motivate even their direct subordinates. Moreover, there are problems regarding employees' loyalty, training, and discipline.

Local employees working for an international joint venture in any country have a conflict of loyalty between the joint venture and the parent company. What aggravates the problem in China is the authority that Chinese partners have on employees' compensation packages. As a result, local employees tend to be loyal only to the Chinese parent company. Most international joint ventures in China have programs in place to train local employees. However, foreign partners frequently find that as soon as their employees receive sufficient training, many leave for another joint venture or local company for higher pay. To a large degree, joint-venture firms have become the training schools for developing management personnel in China. The concept of "face" is part of the traditional Chinese value system, and direct criticism is considered as losing face. Foreign managers are generally reluctant to confront Chinese tradition, leaving employees' disciplinary problems to local Chinese partners. Thus, when workers misbehave, management simply tries to make subordinates admit improper behavior and, through persuasion, correct such behavior on their own initiative.

CHINESE WORKERS
UNDER JAPANESE MANAGEMENT

It is often noted that the main historical root of Chinese management originates from Confucian ethics (Laaksonen, 1988). As such, the characteristics of Chinese management include:

- hierarchical organizational structure, and top-down decision making;
- autocratic approach to interpersonal dealings with subordinates;
- highly personalized style of leadership;
- tight personal control and low degree of delegation of authority; and
- fine division of duties and clear delineation of individual responsibilities.

As stressed by Confucian ethics, Japanese management also places a great importance on seniority and interpersonal relations. However, it encourages and allows the employees to participate in decision making, prefers free-form command to hierarchical command, and draws no rigid demarcation line between individuals' duties and responsibilities.

In short, Japanese management is the opposite of Chinese management in almost every important respect. Hence, the principal sources of problems that Japanese firms have had in China are not only political and economic barriers but also, and perhaps more important, managerial barriers. To gain an insight into problems encountered and solutions sought, we conducted case studies of three Japanese electronics firms, which had built factories in China in the second half of the 1980s. Although the problems that they had experienced were similar, irrespective of the type of production technologies or the size of enterprises, different solutions had been sought. For example, the introduction of Japanese management's group-oriented ideology and practices proved difficult for all three firms, but attempts were made, with varying degrees of conviction, producing different results at the end.

Case 1: Big-J Company

Big-J is a giant multinational company, with more than a quarter of a million employees worldwide and 150 plants overseas. Soon after economic reforms began in China, the company's founder visited Beijing at the invitation of China's then paramount leader Deng Xiaoping. In 1987, the company signed a joint-venture agreement for the manufacture of color television tubes. Premier Li Peng was present at the signing ceremony held at the Great Hall of the People to signify the Chinese government's full support of the venture.

From the outset, the Chinese partners made it clear that they would welcome the transfer of Japanese-style management by Big-J. Thus, adopting the parent company's long-standing policy—"Make people before products"—the joint-venture firm recruited Chinese employees only after stringent aptitude and physical examinations, personal interviews, and background checks. This was followed by several months of intensive indoctrination programs, and then trainees were sent to Japan for an extensive on-the-job training program that lasted nearly half a year.

To date, the company has introduced many traditional Japanese practices, including morning assembly, group-based competition and incentives, continuous improvement programs, and comprehensive welfare programs such as the provision of housing and a kindergarten for the children of workers. The implementation of these practices was based on important lessons that the company had learned through more than thirty years of experience in running global business. Four of the main lessons actually applied to the running of its first joint venture in China were:

- Give overseas operations the best manufacturing technology.
- Let overseas plants fine-tune their manufacturing processes to match the skills of local workers.
- Be a good corporate citizen in every country.
- Keep the number of expatriates down, and groom local managers to take over foreign operations.

Based on these lessons, the company not only transferred advanced technologies to more than fifteen joint ventures that it had since established, but also supplied technical assistance to well over one hundred local enterprises in China. By the end of 1993, its Beijing factory had some 2,600 employees, making more than a million color television tubes a year. Solidly founded on the spirit of equality, sincerity, and mutual benefit, the company also implemented the localization of operations, making the ratio of Japanese to Chinese 1:1 at the managerial level. Ultimately, Big-J plans to build as many as thirty manufacturing plants in China.

Case 2: Medium-J Company

In the mid-1970s, Medium-J opened a factory in Hong Kong to manufacture miniprinters for personal computers and liquid crystal displays (LCD) for pocket-size televisions. In 1984, after nearly ten years of operations in Hong Kong, attracted by cheaper labor and land available right across the Hong Kong/China border, it established a wholly owned subsidiary in Shenzhen Special Economic Zone to shift most of its production work to China. The company now operates two factories in Shenzhen, employing more than 3,500 workers.

"Safety First, Quality First" is the motto that dominates the walls at its Shenzhen factories. Quality control begins at the very start of production process, and all parts purchased from suppliers are inspected. From there on, continuous inspections by both statistical means and human eyes are in place. At the final assembly stage, quality is further checked by rigid statistical tests on about 10 percent of finished products. Moreover, quality control is regarded as the responsibility of each and every employee, and, just as in Japan, strong emphasis is placed on the development, training, and involvement of all workers.

The company has thus introduced the suggestion system to encourage workers, either as a group or as individuals, to submit any ideas for improvement. If the idea is actually implemented by the company, the group receives a bonus for its collective suggestion. Individual suggestions are also highly valued, and a contributor can receive a monetary reward of up to 10 percent of his or her basic monthly pay. However, management has found that the group-oriented quality control circle, widely employed in Japan, does not work with Chinese employees, due largely to cultural differences, and it has not been introduced at their Chinese factories.

The company has a policy of not laying off workers and seldom punishes employees for unintended mistakes on the job.

Instead, it runs various types of on-the-job training programs in order to prevent mistakes and foster desired behaviors among employees. What the company calls "mind training" is also conducted to modify employees' attitudes toward work. The training session is regularly and repeatedly held to teach a set of values considered most important by the Japanese management and, in the end, to implant these group values in the minds of all Chinese employees.

The Japanese national leading Medium-J's China operations has nothing but high praise for the quality of his employees. He claims that, "Of all workers in some twenty of our foreign plants, the Chinese workers here are the most skilled and quickest to learn. In fact, it is even easier to train them than Japanese workers in Japan." He is all for the localization of management. Still, the company has attempted to transfer its home-grown management practices, albeit with some modifications. For example, unlike in Japan, compensations and promotions are not based on seniority but rather on an individual's performance. Nevertheless, as in Japan, the criteria actually used for performance evaluation include not only an individual's productivity and quality of work but also the employee's work attitude, interpersonal skills, and above all, team spirit.

Case 3: Small-J Company

This small, little-known company makes computer accessories. Similar to Medium-J, it moved its entire manufacturing operations in 1989 from Hong Kong, where it had operated for some ten years, to a new factory in Shenzhen. To take advantage of abundant and cheap labor available in the new location, the company introduced only limited automation to its Shenzhen factory. It now employs about 500 females between sixteen and twenty years of age recruited from all over China. The company attempted to introduce the group-oriented ideology to these young employees through a number of measures.

Production targets are only specified for a group and not for each individual worker. If a group fails to meet the target set by the management, all its members are required to work overtime with no extra pay. Furthermore, if any member of the group continues to perform poorly, the group is expected to take the initiative in remedying the situation. In some extreme circumstances, the group is required to make a recommendation to the management to transfer or even dismiss its failing member. Although this may follow the Japanese practice of assigning duties and responsibilities to groups, such a harsh measure is quite contrary to the Japanese management as generally practiced in Japan.

Other Japanese-style management practices, such as collective decision making and implicit control systems, have not taken hold at its wholly owned subsidiary in China. The company regards the management as thinkers, and workers simply as doers. For example, its approach to quality control, which allows little initiative and involvement on the part of employees, can only be considered as "un-Japanese." The managing director at Small-J claims that the quality of products assembled in China is better than anywhere else. He attributes this largely to the tight regulation of quality control systems designed and implemented by the management.

The management's high-handed approach to conflict resolution is not typical of Japanese practice either. In the early 1990s, the pay dispute at a Japanese-run factory in nearby Zhuhai Special Economic Zone triggered labor strikes against many Japanese factories and spread rapidly into Shenzhen. In some companies, strikes lasted for several weeks. At Small-J, however, the industrial action ended only after three hours of work stoppage, when the management unilaterally decided to dismiss anyone who refused to return to work immediately. All but three complied, and they received heavy penalties that included the loss of a half of the monthly bonus normally awarded for a perfect attendance record, which amounted to about 10 percent of the basic wage.

TRANSFER OF MANAGEMENT TO CHINA

In the mid-1980s, when Japan replaced the United States as the world's most competitive nation in business, many linked the achievement to a strategy long adopted by Japanese firms to maximize their human resources. The strategy called for the creation of a corporate culture that promoted group values and spirits and the implementation of intensive socialization processes that incorporated all employees into the organization (Hatvany and Pucik, 1981). In the early 1990s, however, the nation's competitiveness in world markets began to decline. To regain competitiveness, Japan intensified the internationalization of business, and to manage their fast-expanding overseas operations, many Japanese firms doubled their efforts to transfer group-oriented ideology and other features of Japanese-style human resource management (HRM) abroad.

However, the efforts have produced mixed results. For one thing, a higher degree of success has been achieved in manufacturing than service industry, in the management of blue-collar workers than white-collar workers, in "greenfield" operations than mergers and acquisitions (M&A), and in Asia than North America or Western Europe. In addition, the degree of the localization of management differs considerably by industries, modes of operations, and geographical areas. The proportion of Japanese CEOs at overseas subsidiaries tends to be higher in manufacturing than service industry and in "greenfield" than M&A operations; it is also higher in Asia than the West—93 percent in Asia, 82 percent in Western Europe, and 77 percent in North America (Ishida, 1992).

There are several schools of thought that deal with issues related to the transfer of Japanese-style HRM abroad (Beechler and Yang, 1994). Among them are the Culturist School, the Rationalist School, and the Technology-HRM Fit School. Culturalists believe that it is extremely difficult to export wholesale Japanese-style HRM to other countries, such as the United States, because of cultural differences between the homogeneous and collectively oriented Japanese employees and the more heterogeneous and individually oriented foreign employees. Their view implies that the transfer of Japanese-style HRM to a country with a culture similar to Japan is more likely to succeed. By contrast, rationalists believe that Japanese-style HRM is not simply a product of culture; many of its features are attributable to economic necessities that have largely arisen from the nation's industrial development, competitive pressure, and production technologies, and they could be universally employed anywhere in the world. Instead of the universalistic view taken by rationalists, the Technology-HRM Fit School employs a contingency perspective. Its main argument is that different firms have different technologies for products and processes; in order to integrate their hardware with "humanware," they adopt HRM practices that fit the given technologies.

The first two schools have opposing views about the transferability of management across national boundaries. Though both are useful, each has weaknesses in their respective arguments. On the one hand, culturalists tend to be excessively sensitive to cultural differences and fail to note the evolution of HRM practices in Japan as rational responses to the country's domestic economic, social, and political developments as well as international competitive pressures. On the other hand, rationalists tend to neglect the host-country conditions, including culture, that actually govern management transfer from the home country.

Our case studies of three Japanese firms in China seem to suggest that the degree to which the home-country management can be implemented abroad largely depends on the type of production technologies employed at overseas operations. This follows the contingency view put forward by the technology-HRM fit school. Firms engaged in technology-intensive operations, especially those of large size, have a high degree of freedom to put into effect the home-country management system because of their strong bargaining power in the host country. By contrast, those engaged in labor-intensive operations, especially those of small size, do not have such freedom.

In fact, the management of Small-J, which runs small-scale and labor-intensive operations in China, is skeptical about the usefulness of the transfer of its homegrown management practices. By contrast, Big-J's and Medium-J's operations in China are both large in size and technology intensive. Medium-J's wholly owned subsidiary in China generally holds positive views and has selectively transferred Japanese-style management. The management of Big-J, which runs joint ventures in China, holds even more positive views and has implemented many practices of Japanese-style management.

The degree of actual implementation may also vary in accordance with the main advantage that a firm perceives it has in a selected market (Johnson, 1988). Some companies believe that their own management practices will help them attain higher performance than their local competitors. In other words, their perceived advantage is *management centered,* and it is very likely that they stress the employment of the home-country management. If the main advantage is perceived to be *process centered*, then the company is likely to pursue the implementation of the home-country management only selectively. In this case, corporate resources will be devoted more to factory automation. If the advantage is *product centered*, the company is rather indifferent; almost all managerial and other resources are supplied from the home country, and what exists in its overseas operations is merely the screwdriver assembly.

Small-J perceives its main advantage as the low cost, high quality products that it assembles in China, that is, the *product-*

centered advantage; it places little emphasis on the implementation of Japanese-style management. The advantage perceived by Medium-J is *process centered*. The company manufactures quality products through a highly automated process, but its implementation of Japanese-style management in China is low key and selective. Big-J's perceived advantage is clearly *management centered.* Not only has it transferred highly automated manufacturing processes to produce quality products, it has also imported many of the parent company's management ideologies and practices into its Chinese operations.

Over the past decade, the number of Japanese firms operating in China increased drastically, and the firms are faced with the new challenge of determining how much (or how little) Japanese-style management should or can actually be transferred to China. With a relatively short history of operations in China, it is too early to arrive at any definitive answer. The process of management transfer across national boundaries is a complex one; the natural evolution of Japanese-style management itself further compounds difficulty in studying the process. Management in Japan today is in a period of enormous change. As the inherent weaknesses of their traditional style of management are increasingly exposed, Japanese firms are now forced to come to terms with the changing world.

In 1996, Ford, which owns 33 percent of Mazda, named Henry Wallace the president of Mazda. Thus, Japan's fifth largest carmaker became the first major Japanese company to be headed by a non-Japanese in modern times. When asked what was the biggest surprise since arriving at Mazda, Wallace simply said, "Lack of leadership" ("A Scot Tries to Steer Mazda Back to Profit," 1997, p. 22). He was shocked to find a lack of vision and direction at the top. While praising Japan's consensus-building and bottom-up decision-making processes as a strength of Japanese management systems, Wallace was quick to note that when things start going wrong, the company needs someone at the helm who can say, "We're going to change direction. We're going to do some other things." The presence of such a manager from the West deep inside corporate Japan is surely driving the transformation of Japanese management.

This transformation is also driven by cultural and economic changes now taking place within Japan. The cultural underpinnings of Japanese society are shifting toward Western values, as people reassess priorities and goals in their lives. A majority of young workers no longer consider company life the most important. Breaking away from the workaholic lifestyle of the past, more than half of Japanese men in their twenties are now saying that they will not work hard and long just to get promotions, but will instead take it easy and enjoy their own personal lives. Having become acquainted with financial independence, young women are reluctant to give up a carefree lifestyle. Half of all Japanese women today between the ages of twenty-five and twenty-nine are single, and even those who are married are unwilling to have children and get tied down at home.

As a result, the traditional management practices, such as lifetime employment and seniority-based promotion/pay systems, are fast disappearing. In fact, over the past few years, the Japanese government has also been urging upon business executives the necessity of making certain revisions to the traditional salary system that is more favorable for those with longer service. By the end of 1995, the seniority portion of pay increase, which was about 55 percent in the late-1970s, dropped to just under 40 percent. Today, Japanese firms generally favor the performance-based reward system over the seniority-based one. Even trade union officials are saying that lifetime employment and seniority-based systems should not be discussed emotionally at a time when Japan is struggling to get out of the recession. In fact, many companies have already decided to operate with a convergent style of management composed of Japanese and Western characteristics.

Toward the end of the 1980s, Toyota Motor introduced a sweeping restructuring of the company to cast aside decades of hierarchical, group-oriented tradition in favor of individual creativity and initiative. Though it has not jettisoned the ideals of traditional management practices, the company continues to modify them to streamline its management by reshaping the company to resemble an American company. Toyota is just one of many Japanese companies that are introducing new and bold measures to break away from traditional styles of management. Matsushita Electrical Industrial recently announced that the life-time employment system should be altered to allow its employees the freedom to choose whether they want a fixed-term contract or some other arrangements and how they want to receive their salaries and benefits.

As Japanese-style management continues to evolve, its international transferability will become an even more difficult issue to tackle. Japan's direct investment in China is only a recent phenomenon. However, Japanese firms as a group have already accumulated a wealth of experience from operations all around the world that could be applied to their newer ventures in the land of many promises. Indeed, bold experiments are being carried out by Japanese firms operating on Chinese soil. Current evidence suggests that there is not just one but a number of emerging patterns in the transfer of Japanese-style management practices to China.

Chapter 5

Japan at the Crossroads

- Japan's aggressive economic advance into Asia has accelerated the rise of the "ugly" Japanese image. The Japanese must make fundamental changes in the way they think and behave to establish a symbiosis with Asia.
- Japanese culture is composed of a core of indigenous ethos, unique and original, and external layers of alien ideas, borrowed and modified.
- The old Japan is fast disappearing, but the new Japan is not quite born yet. A new generation of Japanese, freed of traditional cultural values, is now leading Japan through yet another of its drastic transformations.

UGLY JAPANESE

Thirty years ago, Japan had the standard of living only half of that of Britain; by 1980, it overtook Britain. And in 1987, it became the world's richest nation, with more than U.S. $44 trillion of national assets compared with the $36 trillion owned by the United States. In September 1991, the country's economy reached the longest and most powerful cycle of expansion in its history. However, the bubble of its booming economy burst soon afterward. Japanese economy has remained flat ever since, with no clear sign of recovery in sight. Alarmed by such a setback, the Japanese are increasingly blaming the government.

Until recently, Japan had a relatively stable and efficient government that had guided the nation toward achieving its postwar economic success. Unfortunately, corruption became endemic in politics. In the general election of 1993, the Japanese finally cast votes of nonconfidence in the government and threw out the Liberal Democratic Party after thirty-eight years of uninterrupted rule. In 1995 and 1996, while their confidence in the government was falling rapidly, Japan was hit hard by three big disasters, of natural and human origin—the "Great Quake" in Kobe, the "Poison Gas Attack" in Tokyo, and the "Outbreak of Epidemic" in Osaka. Although these disasters shocked all and made many realize Japan's vulnerabilities, nowhere was a loss of confidence more apparent than in politics. The disasters in effect served to reveal the government's inability to manage crises.

By autumn 1996, the Liberal Democrats were clawing their way back into power, this time led by Ryutaro Hashimoto. The new prime minister pledged to do nothing short of overhauling Japan's political and economic systems and launched a broad campaign to restore people's confidence. To boost the global competitiveness of lackluster financial firms, his government announced Tokyo's own "Big Bang" financial system reforms. To encourage young people to think independently, bold reforms in the nation's antiquated education system were announced. To improve self-reliance in developing innovative technologies, additional pillars of reforms in research and development (R&D) were proposed. Moreover, Hashimoto advocated a proactive foreign policy, replacing a reactive one that Japan had long maintained simply to respond to *gaiatsu* (pressure from outside).

In short, the prime minister challenged his fellow countrymen with a clear message: "Change or Perish!" Long before his call for change, Japanese firms had increased the pace of international expansion, especially in East Asia. As early as 1977, then-Prime Minister Takeo Fukuda proposed a combination of aid and investment to cement Japan's relations with Asian neighbors.

That was the so-called "Fukuda Doctrine," and its essential idea was that Asia was Japan's natural domain and must be wooed with monetary incentives. Over the last two decades, Japanese businesses have steamrolled Asia and turned it into a vast Japanese backyard.

As a result, many people in the region believe that although Japan failed to conquer Asia during World War II, it has not really quit trying, but simply changed the weapon. Asians worry that Japan is yet again moving toward the creation of the Greater Asia Coprosperity Sphere, the wartime term used to rationalize Japan's military aggression, by economic means. Nationalist-minded or not, many Asians fret that "it's the second Japanese invasion." The invasions hardly seem comparable. Nonetheless, comparisons are made in and by an Asia that cannot dispel memories of Japan's wartime domination.

In *The Voice of Asia* (Mahathir and Ishihara, 1995), originally published in Japanese as *Asia That Can Say "No,"* an outspoken politician, Shintaro Ishihara, willingly admits many mistakes that Japan made during World War II. At the same time, Ishihara urges that instead of dwelling on the past, we need forward-looking, constructive approaches to confront what he calls the paramount reality of the mid-1980s—the retreat of the West and the increasing dynamism of Asia, which presages a period of unprecedented prosperity for Asia. By pouring as much investment and technology as possible into the region, he argues, Japan can atone for the war and can truly play an important role in creating a new economic coprosperity sphere. Still, the suspicion and resentment toward Japan remain deep in the minds of Asians.

According to a survey conducted in 1996 by Japan's daily *Yomiuri Shinbun*, nearly 60 percent of the people polled in China believed Japan was untrustworthy (Spaeth, 1997). In a survey conducted in the spring of 1997 by the official *China Youth Daily*, more than 85 percent of 15,000 young Chinese polled nationwide said that Japan wanted to become a military super-power, and 70 percent saw Japan as a threat to peace in Asia. Even though a majority of them owned Japanese-made electrical appliances, the survey uncovered that the Chinese were even suspicious of Japan's real motives for investing in the mainland, with more than half of the respondents saying that Japanese investors aimed to control China. Moreover, about the same number of them said that the Japanese despised and discriminated against the Chinese ("Atrocity Images Cling to Japan," 1997).

As a follow-up, we conducted an image survey of 300 Japanese and Chinese high school students, ages fifteen to eighteen, in Japan and Hong Kong. Our own survey indeed confirmed that the Hong Kong Chinese respondents, although too young to have been victims of Japan's military occupation of China, were just as fearful of a resurgence of Japan's militarism as their mainland cousins. Although a great majority of Japanese respondents (75 percent) described themselves as peace loving, less than 10 percent of Chinese respondents agreed. Also, the Japanese discrimination against the Chinese reported in *China Youth Daily* does exist in the mind of the young Japanese polled in our survey:

- An overwhelming 86 percent majority of Japanese respondents characterized themselves as hardworking, but only 40 percent of them held the same view about the Chinese.
- The next most striking Japanese characteristic, as perceived by the Japanese themselves, was being polite (66 percent); the Chinese received a lower score of about 50 percent.
- As for intelligence, the score was 63 percent for the Japanese and 33 percent for the Chinese.
- About half of the respondents said that the Japanese were humble, but, here again, they gave a much lower score (13 percent) to the Chinese.

In short, the Chinese were generally regarded by the Japanese youths as lazy, rude, unintelligent, and boastful. The image, either favorable or unfavorable, is created based on preconceived ideas as well as facts. Most of the respondents did not have firsthand knowledge about the Chinese and, thus, their image of the Chinese was largely based on their preconceptions. Quite ironically, however, a similar description of the Chinese was expressed by a well-known Chinese writer, who should know his own people much better than these Japanese teenagers. In his controversial book, *The Ugly Chinaman* (Yang, 1992), Bo Yang described the Chinese as arrogant, uncivilized, stupid, boastful, and so on.

There are few Chinese who really believe that they are stupid people. Looking at their outstanding academic and scientific achievements in America and elsewhere, as well as the fact that most of the wealth in Southeast Asia was created by the overseas Chinese, even Bo Yang must admit that individual Chinese are extraordinarily intelligent. However, as he puts it, the Chinese as a nation are sick. He says, "Chinese people are notorious for quarreling and squabbling among themselves. A Japanese person all by himself is no better than a pig, but three Japanese together are as awesome as a dragon. The Japanese people's ability to cooperate makes then nearly invincible, and in neither commerce nor war can the Chinese ever dream of competing with them (1992, p. 11)."

A survey by *World Executive's Digest* ("Are You Turning Japanese?", 1991) indicated that the general attitude of East Asians toward the Japanese was a mixture of admiration and loathing. The majority of respondents felt that there was much to gain from Japan's economic presence in their country. Yet, nearly two-thirds of them said that too much Japanese presence could lead to a loss of control over their own national economies. They complained that the Japanese made little effort to understand other Asians or to be understood by others. Many of them asserted that the Japanese are arrogant; if there is anyone to blame for the Japanophobia in Asia, it is the Japanese with their "I am OK, You are not OK" attitude. Such an attitude has tainted Japan's standing in Asia and accelerated the rise of the "ugly" Japanese image.

In his book, *The Ugly Japanese* (Bartu, 1992), Asia-based Swiss journalist Friedemann Bartu points out that it is not just the way the cash-rich Japanese tourists or businesses spend their money that causes them to earn the "ugly" title; it is their insensitivity to and disrespect for other cultures. The Japanese are basically sensitive and respectful people. However, once they leave their home country, they do not always behave in accordance with their upbringing. Bartu argues that the government also has a fair share of responsibility. Its checkbook policy of simply throwing money at Asian problems and its self-centered policy for shaping Asia to Japan's own advantage have further contributed to the rise of the image of Japan as the selfish economic aggressor.

"Japan is a fierce dog that bites people," say the authors of *China Can Say "No,"* which became a best-seller in Beijing in 1996 (Song, Qiao, and Zhang, 1996). The authors make the contention that Japan's militarism has not been wiped out. That is partly based on Japan's long-standing refusal to formally apologize for its aggressions before and during World War II. In the spring of 1995, Prime Minister Tomiichi Murayama lobbied for a parliamentary resolution of apology, as part of the fiftieth anniversary of the end of the War, but most members of the Diet opposed his idea. In the end, the Japanese government only issued a bland, meaningless statement of remorse, to which Asians reacted with apprehension and anger.

As the title of a 1989 best-seller (Morita and Ishihara, 1989) suggested, Japan may be becoming a more assertive country that can say "No" to America—the country that can stand up to pressures from the United States on trade and other issues. Yet, it cannot even say "Sorry" to Asians, who suffered from Japanese atrocities during the war. A fuller, more sincere apology would go a long way in establishing a better relationship with Asian neighbors. Certainly, the healing of old scars and the creation of a new image of Japan will require changes in the preconceived ideas held by Asians about the Japanese. This could be achieved through more direct cultural exchange programs designed to help increase mutual understanding at both individual and national levels. More important, it will require changes in the very way that the Japanese themselves think and behave.

A growing number of business leaders in Japan are now arguing that fundamental changes must be made in the way they run business. Privately and publicly, they are saying that economic success should no longer be regarded as the only pursuit for Japan; business firms must establish a symbiosis with Asia and the rest of the world to improve the lives of individuals, even at the expense of corporate profits. Big changes are indeed necessary for Japan to move in the right direction. Still, a strong feeling of cultural uniqueness persists as an enduring characteristic of Japanese society.

JAPAN'S CULTURAL ROOTS

Fundamentally, Japanese culture is characterized by a strong orientation toward borrowing anything from anyone and from anywhere, as long as it serves their purposes. It is often said that Japan behaves similar to a "black hole," which in astrophysics represents an imploding star whose force of gravity is so strong that it sucks in all that comes within its reach. Indeed, throughout its history, Japan always sought out and absorbed knowledge from other countries. However, what they actually did was not plain borrowing, nor was it blind imitation; it was a matter of creative borrowing and organized learning.

The Japanese ingenuity in borrowing from others could be illustrated by the approach they had adopted to introduce progressively value-added products to the world markets (Wee, Lee, and Bambang, 1991). Over the last five decades since the end of World War II, their products development has gone through four stages—imitating, improving, improvising, and inventing. At initial stage of entry into the world market, the Japanese were great imitators. It was quite customary for them to disassemble and then simply copy the superior products purchased from the West. This was the period when made-in-Japan products were known for their poor quality and low price. Then came the period when the Japanese started making some improvements to the products that they had originally copied. Their efforts were concentrated mainly on upgrading the quality of products while keeping the price low.

The third stage of development marked the beginning of real Japanese ingenuity. They started widening the product line by introducing more models and brands in quick succession. This was also the period when Japanese products came to be known for high quality as well as competitive price.

Today, the Japanese are at the stage that is characterized by their quest to invent new products using their own technologies. If successful, Japan could gain an insurmountable lead over the rest of the world in several key industries, ranging from cars and consumer electronics to supercomputers and biotech products.

The Japanese are very proud of their distinct cultural heritage, which they believe separates them from everybody else in the world. The Japanese are convinced that no matter how hard they try, foreigners can never understand their unique way of life. They also say that one cannot be regarded as a "real" Japanese unless he is born of Japanese parents and raised as a Japanese in Japan. There are Westerners in Japan who were born and raised in Japan; many of them can speak, read, and write Japanese just as well as native Japanese. Yet, they are simply labeled as *"henna*

Gaijin" (strange foreigners) because they were not born of Japanese parents. By the same token, even those born of Japanese parents and raised as Japanese are often called *"henna Nihonjin"* (strange Japanese) because they spent too much time outside Japan.

In spite of such a strong feeling of cultural uniqueness, the Japanese culture was actually created through interactions of deeply rooted national ethos with doctrines imported from abroad. The archaeological evidence suggests that the first identifiable native culture appeared in Japan around 8,000 B.C. (Burks, 1981). By the year 300 A.D., the habitants of mixed ethnic origins were unified in culture and in language. Sometime between 200 A.D. and 500 A.D., Japan began to be permeated by influences from the Asian continent. In particular, the discovery of an advanced culture in China and the importation of Chinese ideographs had immediate effects on Japan. What followed was the first program of studies abroad, as the Japanese traveled to China to study arts, sciences, philosophies, architecture, laws, and administration.

The Japanese soon revealed a passion for learning, adopting, and adapting foreign ideas and technologies to their own use. It was a path that they have followed for many centuries since. This is well reflected in the national slogans of Japan:

- *"Japanese Spirit plus Chinese Experience":* Beginning in the mid-sixth century and effectively for the next twelve centuries, Japan was overwhelmingly influenced by the Chinese. Though interspersed with a period of Christian influence (1549-1638) and seclusion during the Tokugawa Era (1603-1867), this long remained the national slogan.
- *"Japanese Spirit plus Western Technologies":* The Meiji Restoration in 1868 and the assertion of Western influence led to the adoption of a new slogan, as the nation became determined to catch up with the West and create a modern society.

- *"Japanese Spirit plus Japanese Technologies":* By the end of the 1960s, after a century of heavy borrowing from the West, Japan caught up with the West and ascended to the rank of world economic superpower. Under this latest slogan, Japan continues to strive to become the world's technological leader by developing innovative technologies on its own.

Although the national slogan changed over the centuries, the Japanese spirit still remains as an important and constant component. The Japanese always made a clear distinction between borrowed and native elements and threw away nothing. Throughout its transformation from a collection of primitive tribes centuries ago into a modern nation-family today, Japan did not turn its back on the roots of its culture, that is, the Japanese spirit, original and unique. One may say that Japanese culture is made of a nonabsorbent indigenous ethos, which is like an igneous rock, and external layers of alien ideas, which are like sedimentary deposits (Burks, 1981).

Long before the advent of overwhelming Chinese influence in the seventh century, Japan went through a vital foundation period to develop the Japanese spirit as its national ethos. The ethos continued to be refined and was crystallized more than 800 hundred years ago during the Kamakura Era (1185-1333). The era coincided with the emergence of feudalism and *bushi* (samurai or warrior) in Japan. Samurai developed the unwritten code of moral principles, *bushido* (the way of samurai), to govern their lives and conduct. *Bushido* started at first as the ideal of this military class that ruled feudal Japan, became an aspiration and inspiration to the nation at large, and eventually evolved into the solid foundation of the Japanese spirit. Originally, *bushido* was a synthesis of three doctrines imported from China in the sixth century—Buddhism, Taoism, and Confucianism.

Buddhism is a religious doctrine that teaches the value of continual refinement toward enlightenment—a goal that is difficult to achieve in one's lifetime. Taoism is a mystical religion that believes in ghosts, spirits, and magics; on the one hand, it places great emphasis on worldly happiness; on the other hand, it values a quiet, secluded, hermitlike life. Confucianism is an ethical doctrine formulated by Confucius more than 2,500 years ago; the Confucian virtues place high priority on reciprocity, justice and honor, hierarchical order, education, and faithfulness. Being an island nation insulated by seas, Japan was physically quite impervious to attack. Consequently, these foreign doctrines were not imposed on the Japanese by force but were accepted willingly. Thus, Japan had ample time to study, digest, and then change them to suit to its own conditions and needs.

Over a period of six centuries after its first introduction from China, the influence of Buddhism in Japan steadily waned. In the twelfth century, Zen was introduced as an attempt to return to the original rigorousness of Buddhism. The ultimate goal pursued by Zen is to attain the essence of the real as summed up in its elegantly simple proposition—"What is, is" (Random, 1987). Zen means meditation, but it soon took on meaning beyond mere contemplation in feudal Japan. With its emphasis on self-reliance, self-discipline, and self-perfection, this new practically Japanese form of Buddhism became a fundamental *bushido* ethic. It taught samurai to be men with a sense of calm trust in fate, quiet submission to the inevitable, stoic endurance and composure in sight of danger or calamity, and scorn for suffering and even death.

Taoism also experienced considerable modifications to emerge as the indigenous Japanese religion—Shintoism. What Buddhism failed to give, Shintoism offered in abundance. While imparting passivity and femininity to the otherwise aggressive and masculine character of samurai, Shintoism thoroughly imbued the samurai with loyalty to their masters and love for the country. The ideal samurai was such a man who would remain loyal to one master, in whose service he would willingly sacrifice his own life. Eventually, the tenets of Shintoism came to represent two predominant features of Japanese emotional life—loyalty and patriotism.

Confucius taught that man did not exist in a vacuum but was inextricably bound to his context, including family, clan, and sovereign. That is to say, man can only define his self by relations to others. Confucianism taught people how they should behave toward each other by observing five important virtues— *jen* (benevolence), *i* (righteousness), *li* (propriety), *chih* (wisdom), and *hsin* (loyalty). Confucianism served as a confirmation of what Japanese instinct had recognized even before the doctrine was introduced from China, and its teachings were particularly well suited to samurai. Nevertheless, after modifications to suit the prevailing conditions in feudal Japan, the central focus of the doctrine shifted from *jen* to *hsin*.

Basically, there are two types of religious or ethical doctrines— the servant of the ruler, and the servant of the ruled. The former serves to justify the ruling power, and the latter aims at helping humanity and offering individual salvation. We could say that Confucianism, in its original form, belongs to the first type, whereas Taoism and Buddhism belong to the second type. However, in Japan, through reinterpretations and modifications, all three doctrines were changed considerably to demonstrate as far as possible the glory of the state and to justify the power of its sovereign.

OLD JAPAN, NEW JAPAN

Samurai took advantage of the teachings of Buddhism, Shintoism, and Confucianism in so far as they concerned their profession of arms. Buddhism taught them self-discipline to develop the character, confidence, and inner self-control needed to face an opponent's blade and death, without flinching. Shintoism imbued them with loyalty to one master and the willingness to sacrifice their own lives, without a moment's hesitation. Confucianism helped them refine their native and traditional virtues to govern their lives and conduct as members of the ruling class. The three doctrines together formed the foundation of *bushido* and taught samurai to be men of righteousness, courage, benevolence, propriety, honor, sincerity, truthfulness, loyalty, and wisdom.

In his widely read classic, *Bushido: The Soul of Japan*, first published in 1905, Inazo Nitobe explains these virtues as follows (Nitobe, 1969):

- *Bushido* begins with righteousness, that is, to know what is right.
- Courage is the outward manifestation of righteousness, that is, to do what is right.
- Benevolence is a tender virtue with feminine gentleness, as compared with a stern virtue of righteousness and courage with masculine uprightness.
- Propriety or politeness is the outward manifestation of benevolence, that is, the act of expressing a high regard for the feelings of others.
- Honor implies a vivid consciousness of personal dignity and worth.
- Sincerity and truthfulness are what make a polite man truly polite, and a courageous man truly courageous, and an honorable man truly honorable. Without sincerity, politeness is simply a farce. Not being truthful is denounced as the dishonorable and shameful act of cowardice.
- Loyalty is a virtue implying homage and fealty to a superior. One's life is to be regarded as the means whereby to serve his master.
- Wisdom is a pursuit for intellectual superiority to be a man of culture, whose actions are solidly based on his full understanding of all the other virtues.

In short, *bushido* dictates that: (1) loyalty assumes a paramount importance in one's life, but he should not sacrifice his own conscience to the capricious will of the master; (2) one must always remain truthful to be an honorable man; (3) one must also be truthful to be a courageous man, who actually does what is right; and (4) one must be sincere to be a polite man, who actually shows his benevolence through a high regard for the feelings of others. With the ideal set by these moral principles, samurai pursued wisdom mainly through the study of philosophy and literature to become a "man of culture." Though considered indispensable, however, wisdom was basically regarded as necessary rather than essential. As a great samurai, Musashi Miyamoto, wrote some 400 years ago in *The Book of Five Rings* (*Gorin no Sho*), the samurai was essentially a "man of action" (Brown et al., 1982).

Besides intellectual training, *bushido* thus stressed constant physical training to improve the technique of swordmanship. The technique must first be mastered by practicing so often that it would be internalized. Only then could one use it without any effort. Mastering the technique is "mind over body"—the mind forcing the body to accept the pain and utter exhaustion of constant practice until the body learns. Using the mastered technique is "body over mind"—the body just doing what it has already learned by heart, without thinking. In other words, to know and to act are one and the same. Knowing without acting is labor lost, and acting without knowing is perilous. It was with this practical end in view that samurai engaged themselves in intellectual and physical training to become "men of culture and action."

In 1870, feudalism was formally abolished in Japan, effectively ending seven centuries of absolute power. With it, the status of *bushido* as the underlying moral principle waned. The findings from our recent survey of high school students in Japan, reported earlier in this chapter, point to this. Although wisdom is still regarded important and is actually pursued to a great extent, there is doubt about other virtues of *bushido*. Based on the majority views, we could only conclude that:

- Japanese appear polite to others, but they lack sincerity. Thus, their outward politeness may simply be dismissed as a farce.
- Japanese may know what is right, but they lack courage to do what is right.
- Japanese can hardly be regarded honorable, for they are not truthful (honest).
- Japanese are not loyal to superiors and groups.

The International Research Center for Japanese Studies in Tokyo recently conducted a survey to examine the image of Japan held by Westerners and the Japanese themselves (Hamaguchi, 1993). Almost all respondents, Westerners and Japanese, agreed on the diligence of Japanese; a great majority of them also agreed on the politeness of Japanese. However, they differed markedly on other points. Westerners described the Japanese as creative, independent, and refined. The Japanese were generally harder on themselves, describing themselves as the opposite— imitative, dependent, and vulgar; in addition, most of them described their own people as insincere. Looking at these survey results from the Japanese perspective, it seems that the current generation of Japanese does not exactly see itself as the gatekeeper of traditional values, as generally represented in *bushido*.

When asked to name what they admired about America, the Japanese polled in a 1992 Time/CNN survey selected the freedom of expression (89 percent), leisure time available to workers (88 percent), respect for family life (87 percent), and the variety of lifestyle (86 percent) as the most admirable aspects of American society that Japan should perhaps emulate (Morrow, 1992). As early as 1989, the Japanese were already spending more on leisure than Americans—29 percent and 27 percent of the total consumer spending, respectively (Rapoport, 1990). The number of Japanese students studying abroad, mostly in the United States, topped 165,000 in 1995—nearly triple the 1987 figure. The number of Japanese who travel overseas has also more than tripled over the past decade. Combined with thousands of Japanese expatriates and their families now living abroad, such exposure to the outside world could only make the Japanese move further away from their traditional values.

As the foundation of Japanese culture, *bushido* long served Japan as its source of light and strength. It was the maker and product of old Japan, but its influence has steadily been on the wane. There are voices, especially among older Japanese, longing for the return of *bushido* as the formative force of the new Japan. However, a great many changes are now taking place within and outside of Japan, making it increasingly difficult for the Japanese to uphold all the old traditional values. Over the past few years, a mountain of economic, political, and social problems exposed Japan's vulnerability and humbled the once confident Japanese. Japan must change, and is changing. However, although the old Japan is fast disappearing, the new Japan is not quite born yet.

At the moment, Japan is down but not out. In spite of numerous setbacks, it may be premature to write off Japan as a world economic superpower. In 1995, Japan accounted for about 18 percent of the world's total economic output and nearly 8 percent of international trade. The nation's economy was then seven times the size of China's, and its gross domestic product (GDP) comprised more than 70 percent of that of all East Asian countries combined. In 1996, Japan's GDP grew 3.5 percent; that was the highest growth rate in the group of seven ("G7") leading industrialized nations, which together accounted for more than two-thirds of the world's combined GDP and about half of all international trade. In the same year, one-quarter of the world's 500 largest corporations were Japanese, including six on the top-ten list ("Global 500: The World's Largest Corporations," 1997).

The Japanese have in the past proved themselves able to cope with changes, internal and external, and turn what are seemingly negative factors into driving forces for positive change. Japan has risen and fallen, but it always rises again. Its modern ascent began with the nineteenth-century reforms of the Meiji Restoration, which was a paradigm of sweeping changes in politics, economy, and society; the goal then was to catch up with the industrialized West. Military defeat in 1945 brought a hard fall, but then came another takeoff and one of the most dramatic half-centuries of progress the world has ever seen; again the goal was to catch up with the West. The 1991 collapse of the bubble economy brought yet another setback. Now Japan is trying to rise again; this time, it has only itself to catch up with (Gibney, 1997). A new generation of Japanese, freed of many traditional values, are more in tune with the outside world and thus more adaptable than their forebears. As Japan stands at the historic crossroads, these younger Japanese now have the task of leading their country through yet another of its drastic transformations.

Chapter 6

Meeting of Two Giants

- Japan is at the pains of correcting mistakes made in their overzealous economic pursuit. There are important lessons from America for Japan to learn to regain its competitive edge.
- With creativity blossoming, Japan may have a good chance to win the technological race and remain as the preeminent economic power in Asia and the world. But the emergence of Greater China poses a serious threat to Japan.
- Even though Japan and China are deeply ambivalent about each other, there are expectations on both sides that by working together as partners, they can gain an equal footing with the West.

LESSONS FROM AMERICA

Throughout the 1980s and for good part of the 1990s, Japanese industrial firms, large and small, moved their production en masse out of Japan and into Asian countries. The main motive of the exodus was to capitalize on the region's cheap labor, land, and locally sourced parts and components. They hoped that the move would lead to greater profitability and competitiveness. Toyota Motors, for example, took several bold measures to increase its manufacturing and marketing presence in Asia. The chief among them was a complementary auto parts scheme announced in 1989, which was designed for the mass production of engines, transmissions, electrical equipment, and steering gears in four different ASEAN countries—Thailand, Indonesia, Philippines, and Malaysia. Some 80 percent of total output was intended to go into vehicles assembled in these countries.

Toyota soon learned that it would take nearly six times as many man-hours to assemble a car in these countries than in Japan. The auto parts rejection rate was nearly 3 percent, compared with less than 1 percent in Japan ("ASEAN: A Challenge That Has to be Faced," 1990). The cost of training local workers to acquire the skills and attitudes necessary to meet the rigid Japanese production standard turned out to be much higher than originally anticipated. The poor quality and reliability of locally sourced parts and components also created unexpected problems when products rolled off the final assembly line. As a result, managers, engineers, and technicians had to be flown in from Japan to fix the problems, often at large expense. In fact, for Toyota and many other Japanese firms, shifting production from Japan's efficient industrial base to less developed countries in Asia proved costly in monetary and nonmonetary terms.

Japan's business competitiveness has long been attributed to its strength in manufacturing systems, especially the integration of production process and research and development (R&D). Typically, managers and engineers spend much of their time on the production floor to offer suggestions for the improvements of products as well as processes. The implementation of continuous improvement programs, such as suggestion systems and quality control circles, is often said to have given an important competitive edge to Japanese firms in the world market. However, as more and more production facilities were moved to foreign locations, some of these key personnel based in Japan began to be deprived of opportunities to observe firsthand the actual process of production.

Considerable sacrifices were also made in R&D. Instead of concentrating on the development of new technologies at home, engineers and technicians were frequently required to make trips abroad just to fix urgent but often minor production problems. This became damaging, especially to those engaged in hi-tech business such as personal computers, where model changes every three months are said to be a "must" just to survive in the fiercely competitive market. To remedy the situation, Sony, NEC, and Matsushita, to name a few, have already scaled down or completely closed some of their overseas production facilities and are returning to Japan to reopen their empty factories or build new ones on Japanese soil.

By bringing back manufacturing to Japan and, with it, managers and engineers, they are hoping to reestablish the integration of production process and R&D and eventually regain their business competitiveness. Now, the weak Japanese yen is also beginning to put a brake on Japanese investment in Asia. The yen, which hit the all-time high of eighty to the U.S. dollar in the spring of 1995, weakened to the level of about 120 by the summer of 1997. A general consensus among economists in Tokyo is that the yen-to-dollar exchange rate should rise to one hundred before Japanese firms would seriously consider investing in the region again. Nonetheless, the earlier exodus of manufacturing industries still haunts this nation, which is beset by economic problems. As recently as March 1995, Nissan Motor's leading factory in Zama, outside Tokyo, became the first Japanese car factory to close since the end of World War II. In the same year, Toyota announced that it would lay off its workers for the first time since 1951.

Perhaps, the pain of their experience in Asia would have been less if they had only paid heed to the warning given by two outspoken Japanese. Almost ten years ago when Japanese industrial firms were feverishly moving their production bases out of Japan, the chairman of Sony, Akio Morita, and the writer-turned-politician, Shintaro Ishihara, published a best-seller titled *Japan That Can Say "NO"* (1989). The book was intended to awaken the Japanese to a new reality that should put Japan on an equal footing with the United States in both business and politics. It was also intended to give an early warning of the "hollowing of Japan," by pointing out that:

- America's huge wealth and dominant position in the world economy was founded on its solid manufacturing.
- As America rapidly shifted much of its manufacturing to overseas locations, the service industry rose to become a more prominent sector of the U.S. economy.
- Americans then began to play "money games" such as M&A (merger and acquisition). Many of the best and the brightest became engaged in the service industry, trying to make a quick buck by simply shifting money from right to left.
- To a large degree, America stopped laboring to make products. This would threaten its once unchallenged position in the world economy.

Morita and Ishihara argued that: in the final analysis, only manufacturing could make money that would really contribute to the accumulation of a nation's wealth; the money thus made should be managed well and used to do more manufacturing; if manufacturing stopped, "money men" would not even have money to manage. The authors warned that Japan should not follow America's path but, instead, should keep their strong manufacturing base at home, especially for the nation's key industries. In fact, however, America has not exactly quit manufacturing. Although moving the manufacturing base for some products overseas, American firms have actually strengthened the manufacturing of hi-tech products at home.

One could perhaps say that while expanding their overseas manufacturing for economic reasons, Japanese firms might have lost their competitive edge in technologies. For example, until very recently, Japan had dominated the world market in the production of memory chips. But the country's semiconductor makers experienced a humiliating defeat to Intel of the United States in the development of new microprocessors. With a renewed determination to revive their manufacturing at home, Japanese firms are now concentrating less on the development of *process-centered* strategy ("how" to make things cheaper and better) and more on the development of *product-centered* strategy ("what" to make). With this shift of focus, they can only hope to gain back their technological leadership and business competitiveness.

There are other important lessons that Japan could learn from America. For the last seven years or so, there has been widespread pessimism about the Japanese economy. In the meantime, the United States recovered from economic recession and went into a long period of growth. One key to the revival of the U.S. economy was deregulation and the freer flow of funds to venture businesses, resulting in the resurgence in competitiveness of American firms. The restructuring wave continues to sweep through corporate America, and it is paying dividends. In 1996, General Motors and Ford moved up to number one and number two, in terms of revenues, on *Fortune*'s "Global 500" list, displacing Japan's three trading giants (Mitsubishi, Mitsui, and Itochu) that had led the list for the previous two years. Moreover, thirty-one of the fifty most profitable companies in the world, including seven of the top ten, were American ("Global 500: The World's Largest Corporations," 1997).

Only two Japanese firms (Toyota Motor and Nippon Life) managed to rank among the fifty most profitable companies. Many Japanese manufacturers underwent difficult streamlining to focus on the bottom line; the efforts paid off, as best reflected by strong upsurges in profitability. In the auto industry in 1996, Toyota and Honda were ranked as the world's fourth and fifth most profitable car makers, respectively—behind General Motors,

Ford, and Chrysler. Likewise, in the electronics industry, Sony earned fourth place, closely followed by Matsushita in sixth place. By contrast, Japan's flagging service industry has made little effort toward restructuring itself.

Of the world's twenty largest commercial and savings banks in 1996, six were Japanese. However, the liquidation of bad loans from the asset-inflated economy of the late 1980s continued to weigh heavily on the performance of Japanese banks. Even the world's largest bank, Bank of Tokyo-Mitsubishi, managed to earn just over $360 million in profits. Though ranked in fourth place on the basis of revenues, America's largest bank, Citicorp, earned ten times more than the Bank of Tokyo-Mitsubishi. In fact, although the combined revenues of Japan's six biggest banks were more than double those of America's "Big Three," their total profits in 1996 were less than a quarter of those earned by these American banks.

In June 1997, as high-profile financial scandals were still unfolding, the Japanese government unveiled a plan for drastic reforms to boost the global competitiveness of the nation's financial system. It is the blueprint for Japan's deregulation program, designed to lure back business that left for less regulated pastures. The program, modeled on London's 1986 "Big Bang," aims at breaking down barriers between banks, brokers, and insurers by: (1) allowing banks to create holding companies through the ownership of securities, trust, insurance, and other financial companies under their umbrella; (2) removing restrictions on the range of business activities conducted by the securities subsidiaries of banks, as well as by the trust banking units of securities firms; and (3) allowing the trade of listed shares outside stock exchanges and cross-entry into banking and insurance business.

Prime Minister Hahimoto stakes much of his reputation as a reformer on the success of the "Big Bang," which he first announced in November 1996. To deal more effectively with financial scandals involving some of Japan's leading banks and securities firms, his government is also calling for harsher penalties for malpractice, more staff for the financial watchdog, and a shift in focus to preventive supervisory checks. The industry watchers doubt if Japan's financial firms have the right stuff to become world-class competitors. Still, they agree that the "Big Bang" is a step in the right direction, which could enhance Tokyo's chance to become one of the world's "Big Three" financial centers, along with London and New York.

JAPAN AND CHINA IN THE TWENTY-FIRST CENTURY

In *Japan's Winning Margins,* Lorriman and Kenjo (1994) advocated that Japan's economic and industrial success was still only in its infancy and it would continue. At the heart of Japan's success, they said, is the Japanese readiness to learn. They noted that there were three elements almost invariably present in Japanese firms but rarely in Western firms: (1) employees committed to self-development through learning, (2) managers committed to coaching employees, and (3) organizations committed to creating an environment conducive to learning at all levels. Indeed, Japan's long cultural tradition of "learning anything from anyone and from anywhere" remains intact today.

Calling these elements Japan's three winning margins, they sum up their arguments with a Japanese saying, *mada-mada korekara-da,* which roughly means "You have not seen everything yet." But, many Japanese are not so sure. Nearly half of the Japanese polled in a recent opinion survey ("Opinion Survey of Japan, U.S., and China," 1997) believed that the United States would remain as the world's most dominant power well into the twenty-first century. It is also noteworthy that just over 30 percent of the respondents considered that China would be the most dominant power in the world. An influential American economist and the author of *Head to Head: The Coming Economic Battle Among Japan, Europe, and America*, Lester Thurow of Massachusetts Institute of Technology (MIT) presents brighter prospects of Japan. He said that with momentum on its side, Japan could be the betting favorite to win the economic honor of owning the twenty-first century (Thurow, 1993).

However, Thurow made this prediction with some reservation because of his doubt about Japan's chance to take over the technological leadership from the West before the turn of the century. He pointed out that in the nineteenth century, Americans were famous for taking British inventions and making them work better than the British did—much as the Japanese have been doing with American inventions for the last twenty-five years or so; after America caught up with Britain at the end of the last century, it eventually learned to be inventive in this century, but it took half a century to do so; likewise, it might take Japan at least another twenty-five years to become the world's technological leader.

Since 1950, Japan received only four Nobel Prizes in sciences and economics, compared to some 170 awarded to the United States. None of the fundamental technological breakthroughs that have changed our modern lives were introduced by Japan. Transistors, industrial robots, color televisions, video recorders, computers, and countless other new products were invented in the West. Yet, the Japanese are the master of the transformation process. They excel in the ability to transform new ideas into commercial products more cheaply, quickly, and effectively than their competitors. By the early 1970s, Japan had caught up with the West in a number of key technologies. Although the country is still the net importer of technologies, it is now masterminding the transfer of its technological expertise to the West and elsewhere.

Nowhere did this become more notable than in the production of memory chips in the 1980s. Japan's dominant position then in this particular production technology, which is undoubtedly vital for future industrial and economic development, prompted the United States and European countries to worry about their increasing dependence on a single country for the supply of memory chips. The former U.S. Secretary of State, Henry Kissinger, echoed this worry when he said, "Japan might become a military superpower because of its potential ability to control the supply of the most advanced semiconductors necessary to drive all hi-tech weapons" (Morita and Ishihara, 1989, p. 20). In a way, the pupil has become the teacher, and the teacher is on his way to becoming the master.

As reflected in its current national slogan, "Japanese Spirit plus Japanese Technology," Japan is determined to develop innovative technologies on its own. In 1993, the country spent nearly U.S. $130 billion on R&D. That placed Japan behind the United States, which spent $230 billion, but still well ahead of third-ranking Germany. On a per capita GDP basis, however, Japan was first, followed by the United States, Germany, France, and Britain. Its per capita scientific/engineering workforce is the largest in the world today—forty-seven per 10,000 as compared with thirty-seven for the United States ("Research & Development," 1996). No longer content to rely on its traditional approach of borrowing Western technologies, Japan is revamping university curricula, building new research facilities and sprucing up old ones, and pouring money into supporting hundreds of promising projects in basic research.

One pillar of the reform plan calls for doubling the number of PhDs in sciences and boosting the number of postdoctoral fellowships from about 2,000 in 1994 to 10,000 by the year 2000. The idea is not only to encourage academic research at universities, but also to build up a pool of highly trained researchers for industries. In 1995, the Education Ministry inaugurated its Centers of Excellence program to provide teams of scientists, regardless of their affiliation, with generous research grants. The Ministry also scrapped regulations that had previously restricted scientists from receiving additional grants from the private or public sector.

Having realized that the real secret to success in today's global markets is creativity, Japanese firms are turning their backs on long-standing traditions to regain competitive edge. In a country where a maxim such as "the nail that sticks up gets hammered down" has long prevailed, nonconformity is in, and freethinkers are popping up all over the workplace. Over the years, many Japanese firms have contracted the "Big Company Disease"; their bloated bureaucracies, endless meetings, and slow decision making were stifling creativity. To foster creativity, some large companies are now resorting to radical changes, cutting entrepreneurial individuals loose from corporate organizations to run their own businesses.

NEC, one of Japan's largest hi-tech companies, for example, has set up programs that solicit new business ideas from employees, choose the most promising ones, and create start-up companies to implement them. The winners get financial, marketing, production, and technology supports from the parent company, but they have free rein to make their own decisions. In 1994, Toshiba introduced flexible working hours in its R&D unit. Initially, the program covered 150 employees; the number was later expanded to 400. The program is intended to turn the chosen ones into creative mavericks, who throw themselves into projects with little restriction on working hours. With all these new experiments and bold explorations on the frontiers of knowledge under way, one can only conclude that Japan actually has a good chance to emerge as a leader in the science and technology race.

Throughout the 1980s, Japan provided the model and much of the capital for other Asian countries' economic development. From 1985 to 1991, two-way trade between Japan and East Asia had more than doubled, amounting to U.S. $158 billion, while Japanese firms had contributed some $25 billion in direct investment to the region (Powell, 1993). A favorite metaphor in Tokyo then was "a flight of geese in V formation," with Japan at its head, followed by Asia's "Four Little Tigers" in the second rank, and "Four Baby Tigers" right behind—all flying in the formation of modernization and picking up industries cast off by the one in front (Grossor, 1990). However, what looked like a neat and well-coordinated arrangement for the region's economic integration under Japanese leadership is increasingly disrupted by the prominence of overseas Chinese.

There are 57 million overseas Chinese—equivalent to the population of Britain. Together with more than 1.2 billion Chinese in the mainland, their combination has come to be known as "Greater China." For the first time since the waves of emigrants left China in the nineteenth and early-twentieth centuries, the overseas Chinese are bonding with the mainland to create something similar to a nation without borders. Linked by common cultural and extensive family ties, it represents a dynamic collaboration of networks that Japan cannot hope to emulate. Some Asia watchers contend that with 53 million overseas Chinese in Asia alone, the economic leadership of Asia will pass from Japan to Greater China in the next century (Naisbitt, 1995; Kraar, 1994).

In 1993, the so-called "three Chinas" (China, Hong Kong, and Taiwan) already accounted for a larger share of world trade than Japan—U.S. $634 billion versus $604 billion; Hong Kong, Taiwan, and Singapore together eclipsed Japan as the primary source of foreign direct investment for Asia—U.S. $26 billion versus $3.7 billion. The overseas Chinese are conservatively estimated to control some $2 trillion in liquid assets, and they have huge influence on the region's economy today. In Indonesia, they represent 4 percent of the population but control 70 percent of the economy. In Thailand and the Philippines, they represent a mere 3 percent of the population but control 60 percent and 70 percent of the economies, respectively.

The overseas Chinese are intensely competitive among themselves. However, when a crisis arises or a greater opportunity presents itself, they will close ranks and cooperate. Though some bristle at being labeled "Chinese" in their adopted countries, culturally and ethnically they retain strong elements of Chinese character. Their economic success has all along been founded on strong family ties, which form the cement of relationships or *guanxi* (connections). So vital is *guanxi* to doing business that virtually every factory in China, for example, has some family or clan connections to explain its location. The overseas Chinese constitute networks of enterprises owned and run by families and clans. These networks are in turn woven together to constitute a huge global Chinese network of networks.

The network has long been anchored in Hong Kong—the world's freest economy and busiest container port, and Asia's second wealthiest economy. It is the fourth largest direct investor in the world. Hong Kong today ranks among the world's five largest banking centers. It is ranked seventh in foreign reserves, and eighth in stock market capitalization. Attracted by low tax rates (16.5 percent for businesses, 15 percent for individuals, 0 percent for capital gains), more than 800 multinational companies have set up their regional headquarters in Hong Kong. As the date for Hong Kong's return to China (July 1, 1997) approached, there were concerns about whether Hong Kong could remain a free and dynamic economy. However, with Beijing's policy of "One Country, Two Systems" and its repeated promise of keeping Hong Kong's economy more or less intact for fifty years after the transfer of sovereignty, expectations are that Hong Kong will continue to play an important role in the global Chinese network.

Greater China combines the cheap labor and natural resources of China, the technical expertise of Taiwan, the financial and managerial know-how of Hong Kong and Singapore, and the access to the growing markets of Indonesia, Malaysia, Thailand,

and Philippines. The overseas Chinese are not only leading the way in driving China's export-oriented economic growth, but also investing heavily in factories, hotels, ports, power plants, and highways to build up the mainland's domestic economy. Greater China links China with the wealth and entrepreneurial drive of the overseas Chinese in Southeast Asia. The countries where they predominate economically have been the prime recipients of Japanese direct investments over the past decades; and Japan's link with the region is expected to grow further, as is China's. Kenneth Courtis, senior economist for Deutsche Bank Capital Markets in Tokyo, once suggested that Chinese and Japanese capitalists were the economic equivalent of oil and vinegar. He said, "They do not really mix, but they complement each other well. The overseas Chinese are the oil—the lubricant that makes deals possible—and the Japanese are the vinegar—the technology, capital, and management that really packs a punch" (Kraar, 1994, p. 40).

ALLIANCE OR RIVALRY?

Geographically, Japan belongs to Asia. However, economically, it has long aligned itself with the West. It was the first non-Western country to enter postindustrial society. It is the only Asian country that holds a membership in the exclusive "G7 Club," formed by the world's seven leading industrialized nations. Yet, the country is set apart from the West by tradition and cultural heritage. As a result, Japan does not seem to be able to decide whether it belongs to Asia or to the West.

A recent survey conducted by Japan's mass-circulation newspaper, "Opinion Survey of Japan, U.S., and China" (1997), suggested that such confusion exists even among Japanese in their twenties and thirties. While 38 percent of them said that Japan belongs to Asia, 39 percent saw Japan more as a member of the industrialized West. Just over 40 percent of all respondents also said that the United States would continue to be Japan's most important economic partner in the coming decades, as compared with about 30 percent expressing the same view about China.

As the main focus of its international trade and investment continues to shift away from the West, Japan will have to identify itself more with Asia. It has even been suggested that Japan should pull out of "G7" to send a strong message to Asian neighbors that it wants to be part of Asia (Naisbitt, 1995). Such a suggestion is too outlandish to be taken seriously by the Japanese. In fact, the World Bank-IMF's September 1997 meetings in Hong Kong highlighted how the recent Asian currency crisis had in fact provided Japan a new opportunity to reexamine the country's identity in relation to Asia. Unlike past meetings, where it had acted as a Western power, Japan was aggressively promoting an Asian agenda. The change reflects powerful common interests among all Asian countries. More than U.S. $100 billion in Japanese direct investment in the region is threatened by the crisis; many of the companies facing heavy debt burdens arising from the drop in Asian currencies are Japanese.

The creation of an Asian bailout fund as part of a financial rescue package has been run very much according to a Japanese plan. Although the plan met a hostile reaction from other G7 countries, Japan persisted. Its continued discussions with leaders from ASEAN, China, and Hong Kong finally caused Americans and Europeans to change their minds. It was also very much owing to Japan's assertive stance that other countries were forced to cave in and give five Asian nations (Japan, Korea, Singapore, Thailand, and Malaysia) voting rights in the IMF to more realistically reflect their economic power. The main lesson that Japan has drawn from the recent turmoil is that its economic interests are so inextricably linked with those of neighboring countries that it should represent Asian interests more aggressively in international groups such as "G7," World Bank, and IMF, which are still dominated by Western powers.

Throughout the modern era, Sino-Japanese relations have been a thorny issue for Japan, as Japan has been for China. For a period of fifty years from 1894 to 1945, the two countries were involved in military conflicts. At the 1895 peace negotiation in Shimonoseki, Hirobumi Ito, Japan's leading statesman of the time, made a telling observation. He said, "China is not an ordinary dragon, but an extraordinarily giant dragon." This image of a giant China became crucial in shaping Japan's relationship with China. However, these two countries are now working together to lead Asia in gaining an equal footing with the industrialized nations of the West.

Japan and China restored diplomatic relations in 1972, leading to the signing of the Peace and Friendship Treaty in 1978. However, even at the height of the Cold War in the 1950s and 1960s, bilateral economic relations existed at an unofficial level between the two countries. As the Sino-Soviet relationships began to deteriorate toward the end of the 1950s and quickly degenerated into a bitter ideological dispute and fierce border clashes, the Chinese increasingly looked elsewhere for economic partnership. Given continuing antipathy to the United States, China turned to Japan and Western Europe. As a result, since the mid-1960s, Japan has been one of China's major trading partners. By the end of 1993, China became Japan's second largest trading partner, behind the United States. In the same year, Japan became China's largest trading partner, moving ahead of Hong Kong for the first time since the end of World War II. China's two-way trade with Japan topped U.S. $62 billion in 1996, with China showing a favorable balance of $19 billion.

As their economic tie became closer through trade, it appeared evident that China's natural and human resources were to be an economic complement to Japan's manufacturing. The Treaty of Shimonoseki signed in 1895 forced China to give Japan the right to open factories and engage in manufacturing on Chinese soil. Today, the Japanese are invited with open arms by the Chinese to do just that. China's main motives for welcoming Japanese investment are to utilize their capital and technology, improve the product quality by using Japanese management know-how, and promote exports to Japan and elsewhere. Japanese firms, for their part, are attracted by China's huge consumer market, availability of relatively inexpensive labor, and abundant natural resources.

Japanese direct investment in China began to accelerate only in the early 1990s, coinciding with the start of Japan's most severe economic recession since the end of World War II. In the spring of 1990, the aggregate number of Japanese-invested projects in China totaled only about 700. Two years later, that increased to nearly 1,900, accounting for about 5 percent of the FDI capital that China had received (Taylor, 1994). If Hong Kong and Taiwan are excluded, Japan now ranks as the biggest foreign investor in China. As China's central government continues to relax restrictions on FDI in tertiary industries such as distribution, transport, real estate, and finance, in addition to the previously favored export-oriented manufacturing industries, Japanese firms are moving aggressively into the service sector to meet the demand of a rapidly expanding consumer market.

Although some Japanese are fearful that such moves would build China into an economic superpower rival, the Chinese are concerned about the real motives behind Japan's aggressive advance into their country. Many believe that Japan is aiming to control China once again, this time economically. To make matters worse, Japanese defense analysts were quoted as saying that Japan, without military strength, could not play an international role commensurate with its economic power. Top officials asserted Japan's peaceful intentions and reiterated that it had no plan to become a military power. Nonetheless, with the quality of its military equipment and advanced technology, Japan indeed has the ability to pose a direct challenge to China's security interests. It is thus inevitable that Japan's economic advance into

China, coupled with its defense buildup, is creating suspicions in the minds of the Chinese.

Despite each side's ambivalence about the other, there are expectations on both sides regarding the benefits accruing from closer Sino-Japanese ties, especially in the light of rising protectionism from the West. From 1993 to 1996, Japan's once huge trade surplus with the world declined by 40 percent to $76 billion. During the same period, the U.S. trade deficit with the world continued to climb, reaching $114 billion in 1996; more than 40 percent, or $48 billion, came from trade with Japan alone. Japan's steadily declining trade surplus was helping the country ease tension with other nations, especially its largest trading partner, the United States. But, even then, economists were quick to point out that Japan's trade surplus could start rising again if America's economy recovered sooner than Japan's.

In fact, after registering a healthy GDP growth rate of 3.5 percent for the year 1996, Japan's economy suffered its sharpest decline since the 1973-1974 oil shock in the April-June 1997 quarter, with GDP shrinking more than 11 percent on an annualized basis. The government downplayed the decrease by saying it was just a reaction to the rush to buy ahead of the 2 percent hike in consumption tax. However, Japan's Economic Planning Agency's report indicated that without the strong jump in exports experienced during these three months, the economy would have shrunk by 16 percent. The report showed that in July 1997, Japan's trade surplus rose by nearly 63 percent, pushing the surplus above the 2.5 percent of GDP that is seen as the danger point. The surplus was boosted mainly by exports of vehicles and electronics to the United States.

Since the mid-1980s, China's international trade has experienced a steady increase. In just four years from 1993 through 1996, its balance of merchandise trade with the world turned around from a deficit of $12 billion to a surplus of $12 billion. In

1996 as a whole, China's surplus with the United States topped $39 billion, with goods shipped through Hong Kong included; that was second only to Japan's. Analysts are predicting that China's surplus with the United States could surpass that of Japan by the end of this decade. As of June 1997, Japan was holding the world's largest foreign exchange reserves—U.S. $222 billion. When the mainland and Hong Kong, now part of China, were combined, China's total foreign exchange reserves stood at $203 billion—nearly three times more than that of the United States. As long as the two countries' trade balance remains in their favor, "Japan bashing" and "China bashing" from the United States are likely to persist or even intensify. There is indeed fear in the West that one day Asia, led by Japan and China, could present a more serious threat than even militaristic Japan did earlier this century.

In the final analysis, a country's competitiveness in business can be maintained if it survives the test of operating in the global markets. Nations vary in the way they strive to achieve the same end. On the one hand, some manage the process by being "aggressive," that is, putting a heavy emphasis on a strong international presence through exports and outward FDI. On the other hand, some nations manage the same process by being "attractive," that is, emphasizing the creation of a domestic environment that is conducive to imports and inward FDI. Generally, a nation focuses on one approach or the other. One could perhaps say that Japan has taken more of the aggressive approach, while China has adopted more of the attractiveness approach. This would make the two countries compatible with each other.

Over the last twenty years, China has been developing the so-called "socialist market economy, with Chinese characteristics." Although that might help the country's economic system become more compatible with Japan's "capitalist market economy, with Japanese features," the gap still exists because of differences in their political ideologies. Beijing has always upheld the tenets of socialism. But hints of a breakthrough in the ideological stance toward capitalist-style, corporate-ownership forms are in the air. At the fifteenth Chinese Communist Party Congress in September 1997, President Jiang Zemin said it did not matter if a mode of ownership was socialist or capitalist, as long as it was conducive to generating wealth for the enterprises and the society." He was merely echoing Deng Xiaoping's theory of hastening economic reforms through the privatization of China's unwieldy state-owned enterprises (SOEs).

Under Jiang's leadership, now confirmed at the Party Congress, Beijing plans to focus on the privatization of 1,000 key SOEs while loosening controls on the remainder of the 304,000 SOEs, allowing them to merge, be sold or, if all else fails, go bankrupt. In a nutshell, China's economic reforms have finally touched the core—the state sector—which is the most difficult to transform. And if the reforms succeed, Japanese and Chinese economies should become even more compatible. In fact, economic relations between Japan and China already reflect a growing complementarity. The Japanese see that China, with its strong and fast-expanding domestic economy, is the market of the future that warrants top-level actions today; Japan needs Chinese help to restructure and revive its faltering economy. The Chinese see that Japan has a lot to offer in terms of capital, technology, and management; China needs Japanese help to achieve its economic reforms and stay on the track of modernization.

In short, Japan and China are being drawn ever closer by the need to achieve their respective goals. And together, the two countries are standing up to new challenges in the world's economy and politics. For example, as the division between Japan and the West over China's entry into the World Trade Organization (WTO) widens, Japan is promoting early accession of China to the WTO. Though such an action in dealing with the West is strengthening the partnership between Japan and China, the economic and political rivalry between them may also intensify.

Japan, a world economic superpower for the last three decades, is starting to convert its hard-earned wealth into political power. China, the foremost political power in Asia today, is turning into an economic giant. Asian countries fear that they might be caught in the rivalry between these two giants. The Sino-Japanese relations must thus be viewed in the context of East Asia.

In a recent study titled "The East Asian Miracle," the World Bank attributed the region's extraordinary economic achievement mainly to the people of East Asia, who study harder, work harder, and save more than people elsewhere (Kraar, 1994, p. 44). Paul Krugman of MIT argues that achievement is no miracle, and if there is anything miraculous about Asian growth, it is a matter of degree, not of kind (Krugman, 1997). According to him, Asian growth is mainly the result of the same things that drive growth everywhere—high rates of saving and investment, high levels of education, and the transfer of large numbers of underemployed peasants into modern sectors. However, students can spend only so many years in school, workers can work only so hard, people can save only so much, and a rapidly developing country eventually runs out of underemployed peasants. As such, he contends, growth is bound to slow down.

Although Krugman argues that Asia's economic miracle never existed, Jeffrey Sachs of Harvard Institute for International Development counterargues that the miracle actually existed, and it is still alive and well (Sachs, 1997). In response to Krugman's view that Asian success has been built mainly on perspiration and not on inspiration, Sachs points out that many countries struggle but few achieve a sustained high rate of growth; Asian success has been built on substantial foundations, such as private-sector orientation, export orientation, and prudent and flexible economic management. In 1950, Asia's share of world GDP was a mere 17 percent; in the past three decades, rapid economic growth propelled it to almost 40 percent. Despite recent turmoil in the region, Sachs places his bet on a swift recovery, followed by many more years of high economic growth. With prudent economic management and flexible response to changes in the global environment, he predicts that Asia's economies will be producing more than half of the world income some time in the early decades of the twenty-first century.

For Japan, it is vital to reflect on and understand fully the extent of its past militarism in order to establish more congruous relationships, economically and politically, with Asia. With help from the Chinese, Japan can improve chances to make friends with its Asian neighbors. And for China, it is vital to get out of their cocoon and establish more open relationships with the world community. With Japanese help, China can improve their chances to make friends with the world. What is being questioned in China today is how Japan wants to live in Asia; what is being questioned in Japan is how China wants to live in the world (Ogura, 1997). For the rest of this century and beyond, Japan's economic advance into China will hold a great many promises for both countries. Although helping each other is no doubt important and beneficial to both countries, Japan and China should also develop the bold, new visions of their relationships with Asia and all the rest of the world for the twenty-first century.

References

Chapter 1

Bartholet, J. (1997). "Life Without Children," *Newsweek*, May 19, p. 18.

Dolan, K.A. (1997). "The Global Power Elite," *Forbes,* July 28.

Fallows, J. (1995). *Looking at the Sun: The Rise of the New East Asian Economic and Political System*, New York: Vintage Books.

Fitzgerald, R. (ed.) (1996). *The State and Economic Development: Lessons from Far East*, Singapore: Toppan.

Halliday, F. (1995). "The Third World and the End of the Cold War." In B. Stallings (ed.) *Global Change, Regional Response: The New International Context of Development*, New York: Cambridge University Press.

"Hong Kong: Up with the Best," (1994). *South China Morning Post,* January 8, p. 13.

Kohut, J. (1994). "Pacific Rim Forum '94: Asia's Economy to Surpass Europe," *South China Morning Post*, October 26, p. B12.

Kristof, N.D. (1993). "Entrepreneurial Energy Sets off a Chinese Boom," *The New York Times,* February 14.

Mahathir, M. and Ishihara, S. (1995). *The Voice of Asia,* Tokyo: Kodansha, p. 16.

Mellor, B. (1993). "A Year for Crowing," *Time International*, February 22, p. 16.

Moffett, S. (1997). "The Nomura Nightmare," *Time*, June 2, p. 23.

Naisbitt, J. (1995). *Megatrends Asia: The Eight Asian Megatrends That are Changing the World*, London: Nicholas Brealey Publishing, pp. viii, xiii.

Orr, D. (1997). "Beijing Can Beat Poverty Before 2020," *South China Morning Post,* September 19, p. 1.

Qian Yingyi and Xu Chenggang (1993). "Why China's Economic Reforms Differ: The M-Form Hierarchy and Entry/Expansion of the Non-State Sector," *Research Program on the Chinese Economy*, paper no. 25, July, London School of Economics.

Sachs, J.D. (1997). "Asia's Miracle Is Alive and Well," *Time*, September 29, p. 36.

"Tokyo Market Faces Cleanup," (1991). *South China Morning Post*, June 26, p. B5.

Vogel, E.F. (1979). *Japan as Number One: Lessons for America*, Cambridge, MA: Harvard University Press.

Chapter 2

Abegglen, J.C. and G. Stalk, Jr. (1985). *Kaisha: The Japanese Corporation*, New York: Basic Books.

Bartholet, J. (1996). "Is Japan Back?" *Newsweek*, July 8, pp. 40-42.

Blakney, R.B. (1980). *The Sayings of Lao Tzu: A New Translation of the Tao Te Ching*, Taipei: Confucius Publishing House.
Caplen, B. (1992). "An Opportunity Too Good to Miss," *Asian Business*, October, pp. 28-34.
Child, J. (1994). *Management in China During the Age of Reform*, New York: Cambridge University Press.
"China's Foreign Trade in 1993 Over U.S. $195 Billion," (1994). *China Economic News*, February 21, p. 12.
Dunning, J.H. (1993). *Multinational Enterprises and the Global Economy*, Wokingham, Berks: Addison-Wesley.
Dunning, J.H. and R. Narula (1994). "Trans-Pacific Foreign Direct Investment and the Investment Development Path: The Record Assessed," *Essays in International Business*, South Carolina: Center for International Education and Research, no. 10, May, 69 pp.
Foo, C.P. and L.K. Cheung (1997). "Privatisation Looms Over State Sector," *China Business Review, South China Morning Post*, September 11, p. 1.
Hofstede, G. (1980). *Culture's Consequences*, Newbury Park, CA: Sage.
Ishida, H. (1992). "Globalization of Japanese Firms and the Frontiers of Human Resource Management" (in Japanese), *Monograph*, Keio Business School, December, vol. 10, no. 1, 14 pps.
"Number of Japanese Factories in U.S. Declines," (1994). *Jetro Denver News*, January/February, p. 1.
Perry, C. (1992). "Shifting Money," *Asian Business*, September, pp. 16-17.
Siu, R.G.H. (1968). *The Man of Many Qualities: A Legacy of the I Ching*, Cambridge, MA: MIT Press.

Chapter 3

Adler, N.J. and N. Campbell (1989). "In Search of Appropriate Methodology: From Outside the People's Republic of China Looking In," *Journal of International Business Studies*, Spring, pp. 61-74.
Brown, B.J., Y. Kashiwagi, W.H. Barrett, and E. Sasagawa (1982). *The Book of Five Rings: The Real Art of Japanese Management* (English translation and commentary of Miyamoto Musashi's *Gorin no Sho*), New York: Bantam Books.
Chen, M. (1995). *Asian Management Systems: Chinese, Japanese, and Korean Styles of Business*, London: Routledge.
Child, J. (1994). *Management in China During the Age of Reform*, New York: Cambridge University Press.
Gao Yuan (1991). *Lure the Tiger Out of the Mountains: The 36 Stratagems of Ancient China*, New York: Simon and Schuster.
Wee, C. H., K.S. Lee, and W.H. Bambang (1991). *Sun Tzu: War and Management*, Singapore: Addison-Wesley.

Chapter 4

Beechler, S. and J.Z. Yang (1994). "The Transfer of Japanese-Style Management to American Subsidiaries: Contingencies, Constraints, and Competencies," *Journal of International Business Studies*, vol. 25, no. 3, pp. 467-491.

Clayton, D. (1995). "Business Basics Put End to Myths," *South China Morning Post*, September 22, p. B14.

Fukuda, K.J. (1988). *Japanese-Style Management Transferred: The Experience of East Asia*, London: Routledge.

Hatvany, N. and V. Pucik (1981). "An Integrated Management System: Lessons from the Japanese Experience," *Academy of Management Review*, vol. 6, pp. 469-480.

Herzberg, F. (1966). *Work and Nature of Man*, Cleveland: The World Publishing.

Hofstede, G. (1980). "Motivation, Leadership, and Organization: Do American Theories Apply Abroad," *Organizational Dynamics*, Summer, pp. 42-43.

Ishida, H. (1992). "Globalization of Japanese Firms and the Frontiers of Human Resource Management" (in Japanese), *Monograph*, Keio Business School, December, vol. 10, no. 1, 14 pp.

Johnson, C. (1988). "Japanese-Style Management in America," *California Management Review*, Summer, pp. 34-45.

Laaksonen, O. (1988). *Management in China During and After Mao*, Berlin: Walter de Gruyter.

Li, L. and C.Y. Tse (1993). "Strategic Solutions to the Problems of Human Resource Management in China's Joint Venture Hotels," paper presented at The Conference on Joint Ventures in East Asia, Bangkok, December.

Maslow, A.H. (1943). "A Theory of Human Motivation," *Psychology Review*, July, pp. 370-396.

"A Scot Tries to Steer Mazda Back to Profit," (1997). *Fortune*, July 7, pp. 22-24.

Vroom, F. (1966). *Work and Motivation*, New York: John Wiley and Sons.

Chapter 5

"Are you turning Japanese?," (1991). *World Executive's Digest*, October.

"Atrocity Images Cling to Japan," (1997). *South China Morning Post*, February 16, p. 5.

Bartu, F. (1992). *The Ugly Japanese*, Singapore: Longman.

Brown, B.J., Y. Kashiwagi, W.H. Barrett, and E. Sasagawa (1982). *The Book of Five Rings: The Real Art of Japanese Management* (English translation and commentary of Miyamoto Musashi's *Gorin no Sho*), New York: Bantam Books.

Burks, A.W. (1981). *Japan: Profile of a Postindustrial Power*, Boulder, CO: Westview.

Gibney, F., Jr. (1997). "In Search of a New Miracle," *Time: Special Issue on the New Japan*, April 18, pp. 16-34.

"Global 500: The World's Largest Corporations," (1997). *Fortune*, August 4, pp. F1-F44.

Hamaguchi, E. (1993). "Japanese Perspective: Japan's Image," *Look Japan*, September, p. 3.

Mahathir, M. and S. Ishihara (1995). "Co-Prosperity in the 21st Century," *The Voice of Asia*, Tokyo: Kodansha.

Morita, A. and S. Ishihara (1989). *Japan That Can Say "NO"* ("NO" to ieru Nihon), in Japanese, Tokyo: Kobunsha.

Morrow, L. (1992). "Japan in the Mind of America," *Time*, February 10, p. 11.

Nitobe, I. (1969). *Bushido: The Soul of Japan* (English edition), Tokyo: Charles E. Tuttle.

Random, M. (1987). *Japan: Strategy of the Unseen*, Northamptonshire, United Kingdom: Aquarian Press.

Rapoport, C. (1990). "How the Japanese Are Changing," *Fortune*, August, pp. 13-22.

Song, A., M. Qiao, and Z. Z. Zhang (1996). *China Can Say "No."* Beijing: China Industrial and Commercial United Press.

Spaeth, A. (1997). "Living in the Asian Family," *Time,* April 28, pp. 62-64.

Wee, C.H., K.S. Lee, and W.H. Bambang (1991). *Sun Tzu: War and Management*, Singapore: Addison-Wesley.

Yang, B. (1992). *The Ugly Chinaman*, Sydney: Allen and Unwin.

Chapter 6

"ASEAN: A Challenge That Has to be Faced," (1990). *Asian Business,* April, pp. 32-33.

"Global 500: The World's Largest Corporations," (1997). *Fortune,* August 4, pp. F1-44.

Grossor, K. (1990). "Economic Interdependence in East Asia: The Global Context," *The Pacific Review*, vol. 3, pp. 1-18.

Kraar, L. (1994). "The New Power in Asia," *Fortune*, October 31, pp. 39-68.

Krugman, P. (1997). "Wrong, It Never Existed," *Time*, September 29, p. 37.

Lorriman, J. and T. Kenjo (1994). *Japan's Winning Margins: The Secrets of Japan's Success*, Oxford, U.K.: Oxford University Press.

Morita, A. and S. Ishihara (1989). *Japan That Can Say "NO"* (*"NO" to ieru Nihon*), in Japanese, Tokyo: Kobun Sha.

Naisbitt, J. (1995). *Megatrends Asia: The Eight Asian Megatrends That Are Changing the World*, London: Nicholas Brealey Publishing.

Ogura, K. (1997). "The Shadow of China," *Time*, April 28, p. 61.

"Opinion Survey of Japan, U.S. and China," (1997). *Mainich Shinbun,* May 17, p. 9.

Powell, B. (1993). "Asia's Power Struggle," *Newsweek*, November 15, pp. 12-15.

"Research & Development," (1996). *Weekly Post,* (Kenkyu Kaihatsu), in Japanese, April 19, pp. 30-42.

Sachs, J.D. (1997). "Asia's Miracle Is Alive and Well," *Time*, September 29, p. 36.

Taylor, R. (1994). "Japan's Role in China's Economic Transformation Since 1978," *Journal of Far Eastern Business*, vol. 1, no. 2, pp. 13-33.

Thurow, L. (1993). *Head to Head: The Coming Economic Battle Among Japan, Europe, and America*, New York: Warner Books.

Selected Readings

Abegglen, J.C. and G. Stalk, Jr. (1985). *Kaisha: The Japanese Corporation*, New York: Basic Books.

Adler, N.J. and N. Campbell (1989). "In Search of Appropriate Methodolody: From Outside the People's Republic of China Looking In," *Journal of International Business Studies*, Spring, pp. 61-74.

Bartu, F. (1992). *The Ugly Japanese*, Singapore: Longman.

Burks, A.W. (1981). *Japan: The Profile of a Postindustrial Power*, Boulder, CO: Westview.

Chen, M. (1995). *Asian Management Systems: Chinese, Japanese, and Korean Styles of Business*, London: Routledge.

Child, J. (1994). *Management in China During the Age of Reform*, New York: Cambridge University Press.

Dunning, J.H. and R. Narula (1994). "Trans-Pacific Foreign Direct Investment and the Investment Development Path: The Record Assessed," *Essays in International Business*, Columbia, South Carolina: Center for International Education and Research, May, 69 pp.

Fallows, J. (1995). *Looking at the Sun: The Rise of the New East Asian Economic and Political System*, New York: Vintage Books.

Fitzgerald, R. (ed.) (1996). *The State and Economic Development: Lessons from Far East*, Singapore: Toppan.

Fukuda, K.J. (1988). *Japanese-Style Management Transferred: The Experience of East Asia*, London: Routledge.

Hofstede, G. (1980). *Culture's Consequences*, Newbury Park, CA: Sage.

Kraar, L. (1994). "The New Power in Asia," *Fortune*, October 31, pp. 39-68.

Laaksonen, O. (1988). *Management in China During and After Mao*, Berlin: Walter de Gruyter.

Lorriman, J. and T. Kenjo (1994). *Japan's Winning Margins: The Secrets of Japan's Success*, Oxford, England: Oxford University Press.

Mahathir, M. and S. Ishihara (1995). *The Voice of Asia*, Tokyo: Kodansha.

Miyamoto, M. (circa 1645). *Gorin no Sho,* I. Watanabe (ed.) 1995. Tokyo: Iwanami Bunko.

Morita, A. and S. Ishihara (1989). *Japan That Can Say "NO"* ("NO" to ieru Nihon), in Japanese, Tokyo: Kobunsha.

Naisbitt, J. (1995). *Megatrends Asia: The Eight Asian Megatrends That Are Changing the World*, London: Nicholas Brealey.

Nitobe, I. (1969). *Bushido: The Soul of Japan* (English edition), Tokyo: Charles E. Tuttle.

Taylor, R. (1994). "Japan's Role in China's Economic Transformation Since 1978," *Journal of Far Eastern Business*, vol. 1, no. 2, pp. 13-33.

Thurow, L. (1993). *Head to Head: The Coming Economic Battle Among Japan, Europe, and America*, New York: Warner Books.

Wee, C.H., K.S. Lee, and W.H. Bambang (1991). *Sun Tzu: War and Management*, Singapore: Addison-Wesley.

Yang, B. (1992). *The Ugly Chinaman*, Sydney: Allen and Unwin.

Index

Order Your Own Copy of
This Important Book for Your Personal Library!

JAPAN AND CHINA
The Meeting of Asia's Economic Giants

_____ in hardbound at $49.95 (ISBN: 0-7890-0417-8)

COST OF BOOKS _____

OUTSIDE USA/CANADA/
MEXICO: ADD 20% _____

POSTAGE & HANDLING _____
(US: $3.00 for first book & $1.25
for each additional book)
Outside US: $4.75 for first book
& $1.75 for each additional book)

SUBTOTAL _____

IN CANADA: ADD 7% GST _____

STATE TAX _____
(NY, OH & MN residents, please
add appropriate local sales tax)

FINAL TOTAL _____
(If paying in Canadian funds,
convert using the current
exchange rate. UNESCO
coupons welcome.)

☐ **BILL ME LATER:** ($5 service charge will be added)
(Bill-me option is good on US/Canada/Mexico orders only;
not good to jobbers, wholesalers, or subscription agencies.)

☐ Check here if billing address is different from
shipping address and attach purchase order and
billing address information.

Signature _____

☐ **PAYMENT ENCLOSED: $** _____

☐ **PLEASE CHARGE TO MY CREDIT CARD.**

☐ Visa ☐ MasterCard ☐ AmEx ☐ Discover
☐ Diner's Club
Account # _____

Exp. Date _____

Signature _____

Prices in US dollars and subject to change without notice.

NAME _____

INSTITUTION _____

ADDRESS _____

CITY _____

STATE/ZIP _____

COUNTRY _____ COUNTY (NY residents only) _____

TEL _____ FAX _____

E-MAIL_____
May we use your e-mail address for confirmations and other types of information? ☐ Yes   ☐ No

Order From Your Local Bookstore or Directly From
The Haworth Press, Inc.
10 Alice Street, Binghamton, New York 13904-1580 • USA
TELEPHONE: 1-800-HAWORTH (1-800-429-6784) / Outside US/Canada: (607) 722-5857
FAX: 1-800-895-0582 / Outside US/Canada: (607) 772-6362
E-mail: getinfo@haworthpressinc.com
PLEASE PHOTOCOPY THIS FORM FOR YOUR PERSONAL USE.

BOF96

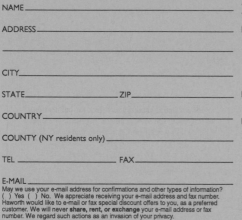